AS I FIND IT, BOOK III

DESCENDANTS OF THE SEAL (SEALE), BARLOW, PITTS, SOUTHWORTH & TAYLOR FAMILIES OF CAROLINE COUNTY, VIRGINIA

RUTH E. PITTS

RoseDog Books

PITTSBURGH, PENNSYLVANIA 15238

RoseDog Books
585 Alpha Drive
Suite 103
Pittsburgh, PA 15238
Visit our website at *www.rosedogbookstore.com*

ISBN: 978-1-6491-3009-9
eISBN: 978-1-6491-3024-2

AS I FIND IT, BOOK III
CORRECTIONS
& ADDITIONAL INFORMATION

The book, AS I FIND IT, was published in September 2003; AS I FIND IT, PART II, was published in November 2006. This, the third book, AS I FIND IT, PART III, of the Seal, Barlow, Pitts, Southworth, and Taylor families, is being published to add new information and update the first two books on births, marriages and deaths that occurred since 2006.

CORRECTIONS:

If the word "Correction" is noted beside an entry, it means a correction has been made to that entry.

ADDITIONAL INFORMATION:

All other information in this book is new material added through further research since the first two books were published.

ABBREVIATIONS:

- b.   born
- d.   death
- m.   marriage
- c.   about

This book is dedicated in memory of
Anne Jackson Morledge, a dear friend
and source of inspiration.

*"A friend is someone who knows the
song in your heart and can sing it
back to you when you have
forgotten the words."*

Acknowledgements

A special thanks to Karen Watts
Covington in making this journey
with me through her contribution
in seeing this book to its fruition.

*"It is the job that is never started
that takes longest to finish."*

THE SEAL (SEALE)-BARLOW-PITTS-SOUTHWORTH-TAYLOR

Families of Caroline County, Virginia

I have spent 26 years (1993-2020) in the genealogical research tracing our line of descent; it has been frustrating at times, but very rewarding also.

In tracing our family history, I started writing down what I already knew, concentrating on names and dates of births, marriages, deaths, looking on the backs of old photos, and reading other documents about family members. I visited cemeteries, searched church records, and read genealogical research guides at the libraries. I talked to the "few" older relatives still living, and people who knew or had lived for a long time. Sometimes they could give a "storehouse" of information on the family even though they were not related.

I visited historical societies in other states (KY, UT, SC) to gather information on descendants that had moved from Virginia, especially early descendants.

As one guide says, "research is a step-by-step process, with each new fact requiring analysis".

I want to extend a thank you to family members and other professional researchers that helped me in so many ways to gather all the information for the books published. I hope you will enjoy reading about your family connection(s) and find it useful as you think back on your heritage.

RUTH E. PITTS

APRIL 2020

TABLE OF CONTENTS

WHY DO WE SEARCH

Why do we spend our time, they say,
Looking for forefathers hidden away.
They'd never believe the places we look!
Attics and trunks and every old nook.
Wheezing and sneezing covered with grime,
Searching for facts from an earlier time.
In bibles, records, letter and bills,
Censuses, papers, photos and wills,
Courthouses, churches and graveyards too,
Ferreting out every possible clue.
To finding out who, what, where, and when,
Was important to our folks back then.
We chat with all our kith and kin,
And then we review just where we've been.
Some folks say we're a little bit crazy,
Looking for things that are now quite hazy.
We write those letters and then we wait,
Hoping to locate a certain date.
The facts begin to trickle in,
They fill our drawers and every bin.
We finally have to buy some files,
Just to organize all the piles.
We must be faced with an affliction,
That's called genealogy addiction,
Yet, we never seem to get enough,
Of that old family history stuff.

Reprinted from PasTimes, St Cloud Area Genealogist, Inc. September 1991

A good family is like an umbrella—it won't keep you from being spattered by the rainstorms of life, but it won't let you get completely drenched either.

Providence Baptist Church

When Providence Baptist Church was organized in 1837, church membership numbered as high as 150; by 1975, membership totaled 47. Like most old churches, Providence was once strict on its members. According to church records, a couple was put out of the church for stealing a slave. The records show, too, that a large number of slaves were baptized and were members of Providence. Providence has an interesting historical point. The late Dr. George W. Beale said "the earliest Sunday School of which we have any knowledge in Virginia was gathered where Providence Church later built its meeting house". Some of our ancestors and their descendants held membership in this church from late 1800 to 1915.

Today, Providence Baptist Church no longer exists. Mrs Sallie Selph, the Clerk for 45 years and its last remaining officer, held that post until she signed the papers transferring ownership to the Bowling Green congregation. What happened to Providence she said is that the battle was lost to attrition. The old church which was located on Rt 734 (off Sparta Road) is now Grace Baptist Church.

Some other interesting facts taken from the church minutes are as follows:

- James F Brooks was dismissed from the church in April 1852.
- William H Taylor was baptized 29 August 1847.
- Burton Lewis Taylor erased December 1886.
- Mordicai E Taylor baptized on 27 August 1847.
- Lucy M Taylor received by letter September 1856.
- C B Southworth dropped from roll 27 July 1878.
- John L Taylor was baptized in September 1879.
- Alberta S Taylor Noel erased 3 October 1885.
- Burton Lewis Taylor erased December 1886.
- Burton L Taylor restored in September 1887.
- Laura A Poats dismissed by letter in 1889.
- Lucy Jane Taylor dismissed by letter in June 1890.
- Frank L Taylor dismissed by letter in June 1891.
- Lucy M Taylor dismissed by letter in 1892.
- Frank L Taylor excluded in 1892.
- Frank L Taylor restored in September 1895.
- Virginia Taylor Beazley died in April 1896.
- Uriah Taylor died in 1896.
- Hiram Taylor died 24 December 1897.
- Bettie Carr Pitts dismissed by letter in 1898.
- T H Pitts was a member in April 1903.
- Robert Pitts – 1904.
- Manley Taylor was a member in September 1909.
- Harry Taylor was a member in September 1909.
- John Edward (Ned) Taylor was a member in September 1909.
- Myrtle Taylor was a member in September 1909.

- Ollie Taylor was a member in September 1909.

- Effie Pitts Crowell was a member in September 1909.

- Kate Taylor was baptized in May 1912.

- John Pitts was a member in 1917.

- Roy Pitts was a member in 1917.

- Carroll Pitts came by statement in October 1922.

- Bettie C Pitts died 14 February 1918.

Edmund Pendleton High School

One Room School House

THE SEALE FAMILY CORRECTIONS & ADDITIONAL INFORMATION

Page 39   Anthony Seale, b. 1659 in Westmoreland Co, VA, d. 1726 in King George Co, VA; m. in 1684 to Dorothy Hanna Hughes, b. 1663, d. 1703. Their issue:

1. John Seale, b. 1686
2. Cornelius Seale, b. 1687
3. Thomas Seale, b. 1688, d. 1750
4. James Seale, b. 1689
5. Hannah Seale, b. 1690
6. Elizabeth Seale, b. 1691
7. David Seale
8. Anthony Seale, b. 1695 in Essex Co, VA, d. 1781
9. Charles Seale, b. 1700 in Essex Co, VA, d. 1737

Page 39   David Seale, b. 1694 in King George Co, VA, d. Apr 1755 in King George Co, VA; m. Apr 1724 to Jael Glendening, b. 1698, d. 13 Oct 1761 in King George Co, VA. Their issue:

1. William Seale, b. c. 1730, d. 1815
2. James Seale, b. 1734, d. 1823 in King George Co, VA

3. Eleanor Seale, b. 1735 in King George Co, VA, d. 1735 in King George Co, VA
4. Anthony Seale, b. Jun 1744 in King George Co, VA, d. 1822
5. David Seale II

Page 39
Correction

David Seale II, b. 1745 in King George Co, VA, d. 11 Dec 1820 in Caroline Co, VA; m. c. 1770 in King George Co, VA to Isabella "Figg", b. 1745, d. 1825. David served in the War of 1812.
Their issue:

1. Bennett Seal(e), b. 1776 in Caroline Co, VA, d. 1850; m. 8 Dec 1800 to M Elizabeth Seal
2. Thomas Seal(e), b. c. 1777, d. 1840
3. Patsy (Polly) Seal(e), b. c. 1780, d. ___________
4. James Seal(e), b. 9 May 1782 in Caroline Co, VA, d. 1859
5. Edward Cary Seal(e) Tuck, b. c. 1785 in Caroline Co, VA, d. c. 1881
6. John H Seal(e), b. 1789, d. 16 Nov 1858 in Caroline Co, VA
7. Clementine (Claudia) Seal(e), b. c. 1793, d. ___________
8. Nancy Edwards Seal(e), b. c. 1795 in Caroline Co, VA, d. 1860; m. 4 Jan 1819 to William Lewis Edmundson
9. David Seal(e) III, b. c. 31 Jul ______, d. 1818

Page 40

Hester Seal(e) was born 21 Oct 1834

Page 42
Correction

Marcia Anne Seal(e), m. (1) "Favell Francis"

Page 42
Correction

Frances Lillian Seal should read "Florence Lillian Seal(e)"

Page 42   Betty Harper Wyatt died 2 Jul 2013. She is buried in St John's Episcopal Church Cemetery, Hampton, VA. Betty is the daughter of Florence Seal(e) Harper.

Page 42   Ira Blanche Seal should read "Ida Blanche Seal(e)"
Correction

Page 43   Edmonia Churchill Seal(e), m. (1) Charles Lusien; (2) Anton Van Haagen, b. 1822, d. 1899. Issue of second marriage:

1.   Hermania Van Haagen, b. 1852
2.   John C Van Haagen, b. 1862
3.   Rebecca Van Haagen, b. 1864
4.   Henry E V Van Haagen, b. 1865

Page 47   (Should Follow Will of John Seal)

COPY

We, the undersigned, do hereby agree and bind ourselves that Catherine Southworth shall come in and have an equal share of the estate of the late John Seal, both real and personal, provided that Achilles Southworth shall agree that the said Catherine's share or portion of the said John Seal's estate shall be put in the hands of Griffin Garnett or some other person named and selected as Trustee for the said Catherine and her children, which share or portion that said Catherine shall have the benefit and use of during her natural life, and at her death to be divided equally among her children or their legal representatives. In testimony whereof we do hereby set our names this 18th day of November 1856.

WITNESS

Robt Hudgin, as to F. Seal	Fred Seal (SEAL)
Griffin T. Garnett	W. P. Martin (SEAL)
(as to W. P. Martin	John Wharton (SEAL)
Wm Blanton)	William Barlow (SEAL)
TEST: Henry Wrians	Festus Seal (SEAL)
	Franklin M. Kelly (SEAL)

Barlow-Pitts-Taylor Reunion, 1939

THE BARLOW FAMILY CORRECTIONS & ADDITIONAL INFORMATION

Page 65   William I Barlow, b. 1503, d. 1581; m. Katherine Hale, b. 1509, d. 1592. They lived in Barlow Hale at Barlow Moor, which was near Manchester, England. They died in Manchester, England. Their issue:

1. William I Barlow II
2. Arthur Barlow, b. 1541, d. 1602. He was an English navigator; he explored the coast of NC in 1584.
3. Mary Barlow
4. Elizabeth Barlow

Page 65   William I Barlow II, b. 1538, d. 1616; m. Elizabeth Rishton in 1559. William was a tradesman in Winslow/Creshire, England. Their issue:

1. Edward Barlow
2. Thomas James Barlow
3. Katherine Barlow
4. William Barlow

Page 65   Edward Barlow, b. 1561, d. 19 Mar 1620; m. 20 Dec 1592 to
                 Joan Rishton, b. 1561, d. 1619, in Sussex, England. Edward was
                 born in Winslow/Creshire, England. They are buried in St Michael
                 Parish in England. Their issue:

1. Roger Barlow, b. 1600
2. Henry B Barlow
3. James Barlow
4. Katherine Barlow
5. Anne Barlow

Inspired by their uncle, Arthur Barlow, Henry and his brother, Roger, after their father's death, with their cousins, Ralph and Thomas, came to America aboard CPT Arthur Barlow's ship. They settled in Accawamack County on the Eastern Shore of Virginia in 1631. They were well-established in America by 1633. They were important figures in the mid 1600's in VA; each is mentioned many times in the court records as Juror, Trustee, and other appointees of the court.

Page 65   Henry B Barlow, b. 1601, d. 1657; m. in 1628 to Elizabeth Parker.
                 Henry died in Northampton County, VA at the age of 56. Their issue:

1   Henry James Barlow
2. Ann Barlow
3. Ralph Barlow

Page 65   Henry James Barlow, b. 1631, d. 1701; m. in 1665 to Margaret
                 Balfour, b. 1638, d. 1708. Their issue:

1. Henry James Barlow Jr
2. Robert Barlow

3. Anne Barlow

4. Roger Barlow

Page 65

Henry James Barlow Jr, b. 1673, d. 1761; m. in 1695 to Katherine E Baker, b. ___________, d. ___________ . Henry followed in the footsteps of his father as the minister of Hunger Parish. In 1729, he was appointed by the Bishop of London to serve Lynnhaven Parish, which he did until Oct 1747. At that time, he returned to Hunger Parrish in Northampton Co, VA, where he remained until his death in 1761. Henry and Katherine died in Northampton Co and are buried in Hunger Parish. Their issue:

1. Thomas Barlow

2. Elizabeth Barlow

3. Edward Barlow

4. Joseph Barlow

5. William Barlow

Page 65

Thomas Barlow, b. 1697, d. 1781, m. in 1718 to Sarah Baker, b. 1699, d. 1768 (a niece of his mother, Katherine Baker). They lived in King & Queen Co where Sarah was from. Thomas was a minister and farmer in King & Queen Co; they owned 63 acres of land in that county. In 1727, Caroline Co was formed from a part of King & Queen Co, VA. This included the land that Thomas and Sarah owned. Their issue:

1. Henry Benjamin Barlow

2. William Barlow

NOTE: Henry and William fought in the French and Indian War under COL Humphrey Hill of William Byrd's Co of the 2nd Virginia

Militia. COL Byrd solicited men from his 2nd Virginia Militia Co to join MAJ George Washington in the march to the Forks of the Ohio River, and William and Henry volunteered to join the campaign. After the war, William remained with COL Hill as caretaker of his farm and received a 50-acre grant for his services as recommended by MAJ Washington.

Page 65

Henry Benjamin Barlow, b. 1726 and raised in Caroline Co, VA, d. 1815 in Scott Co, KY. He m. in 1743 to Judith Livingston, b. 1727, d. 1815. In 1790, he and Judith moved to Scott Co, KY, with some of their children. They are buried in Scott Co, KY. Their issue:

1. Robert Thomas Barlow
2. James L Barlow
3. Mildred (Millie) Barlow
4. Elizabeth Barlow
5. Henry Benjamin Barlow Jr
6. Frances Barlow
7. William Barlow

Page 65

Robert Thomas Barlow, b. 1744, d. 1825 in Caroline Co, VA; m. in 1765 to Jane Burruss, b. 1748, d. 1791. They lived in Caroline Co, VA. Robert was a PVT in the Virginia Militia and served in the American Revolutionary War. Their issue:

1. Henry Thomas Barlow
2. Sarah Barlow
3. James Barlow
4. John Barlow

Henry Thomas Barlow, b. 25 Aug 1765 in Caroline Co, VA, d. 30 Jan 1825; m.(1) in 1788 to Lucy Lancaster, b. 1767, d. 1791. In 1793, Thomas moved to Wilkes Co, NC. There he met and m. (2) on 28 Jan 1794 to Susan Childs Isbell, b. 2 Jan 1777 in NC, d. 12 Jan 1863 in Georgetown, KY. Thomas and Susan moved to Scott Co, KY, to land received in a land grant by his uncle, William Barlow. Thomas Barlow was engaged in the Battle of Yorktown, VA, serving under GEN Lafayette. Thomas and Susan died in KY and are buried in Scott Co, KY. Issue by first marriage:

1. Thomas Barlow
2. James Barlow
3. Robert Barlow
4. John William Barlow

Issue by second marriage:

1. Hastings Livingston Barlow
2. Nancy Martin Barlow
3. Cynthia Childs Barlow
4. Lavinia Waller Barlow
5. Martin Boler Barlow
6. Thomas Jefferson Barlow
7. Polly Isbell Barlow
8. William Henry Harrison Barlow
9. James Madison Anderson Barlow

John William Barlow, b. Sep 1791 in Caroline Co, VA, d. 1867 in Frankfort, KY; m. 8 Aug 1808 in Caroline Co, VA, to Minnie Barker. (NOTE: Some records have shown her name as MILLIE BUTLER.), b. 1791, d. 1869. John William stated in a reply to a Chancery suit in Caroline Co, VA, in Sep 1821 that he had been willed one-fourth of the estate of his grandmother, Sina Burruss (mother of Jane Burruss Barlow), by her last will in Oct 1800, and that he had lived as an adult with his grandfather, Robert Barlow, and that his father had moved to the western county. Sometime prior to the Civil War, William and Minnie joined their other children in KY. John William and Minnie are buried near Frankfort, KY. Their son, William Edward Barlow, remained in VA on family land. Their issue:

1.   Lucy Polly Barlow
2.   William Edward Barlow
3.   Susan Barlow
4.   John Barlow
5.   James Barlow
6.   Robert Barlow

Page 65   Hastings Livingston Barlow, b. 27 Mar 1795 in Georgetown, KY, d. 1823

Nancy Martin Barlow, b. 10 Sep 1796 in Georgetown, KY, d. 21 Jun 1834; m. J W McCann. No issue.

Cynthia Childs Barlow, b. 8 Jul 1798 in Georgetown, KY, d. 1877; m. D Winthrop (Humphrey) Foote. They had three children.

Lavinia Waller Barlow, b. 7 Jul 1800 in Georgetown, KY, d. 1870; m. Robert W Carleton. They had three children.

Martin Boler Barlow, b. 12 Nov 1802 in Scott Co, KY, d. 21 Aug 1871 in IL; m. (1) 16 Mar 1830 in Bourbon Co, KY, to Frances (Fannie) Ann Cantrill, b. 1802, d. 1846; m. (2) 10 Nov 1836 in Monroe, MO, to Elizabeth Dearing(s), b. 1816, d. 27 Apr 1852. Issue by first marriage:

1. Mary Barlow, b. 1832 in KY, d. 1912
2. Joseph Thomas Barlow

Issue by second marriage:

1. James M Barlow, b. 6 Nov 1837 in Monroe, MO, d. 1920
2. Frances Ann Barlow, b. 24 Apr 1839 in Paris, MO, d. 1917;
   m. ___________ Journey
3. William H Barlow, b. 1845 in Monroe, MO, d. ___________
4. Mildred L Barlow, b. 1846 in Monroe, MO, d. ___________;
   m. ___________ Wright

Joseph Thomas Barlow, Farmer, b. 31 Jan 1834 in Boone Co, MO, d. 1912; m. 1855 to Annie R Lydick, b. ___________, d. ___________. Their issue:

1. Lelia Barlow, m. J B Ammerman
2. Mollie Barlow, m. J T Hill of TX
3. Bettie Barlow, m. John Stamps of TX
4. Ella Barlow
5. Frankie Barlow

Page 65   Thomas Jefferson Barlow, b. 26 Dec 1804 in Georgetown, KY, d. 1873; m. Millie Cantrill

Mary Isbell (Polly) Barlow, b. 24 Apr 1807 in Georgetown, KY, d. 1881; m. John F Cantrill

William Henry Harrison Barlow, b. 3 Sep 1809 in Georgetown, KY, d. 14 Dec 1887 in Lexington KY; m. Louisa J Allgaier

James Madison Anderson Barlow, b. 9 Jul 1812 in Georgetown, KY, d. 1893; m. E H Barlow

Page 65   James L Barlow, b. 1747 in Caroline Co, VA, d. 1828 in LA; m. Lucy Edwards, b. 1758, d. 1828. Their issue:

1.   William Barlow, b. 1778, d. 1818
2.   Lawrence Dunmore Barlow, b. 1780, d. 1850
3.   Nathaniel Barlow, b. 1781, d. 1781
4.   Thomas Barlow, b. 1783, d. 1820
5.   Elizabeth Barlow, b. 1785, d. 1865
6.   Lucinda Barlow, b. 1787, d. c. 1820
7.   Lucretia Barlow, b. 1790, d. 1857
8.   Mary Polly Barlow, b. 1794, d. ____________

Page 65   Mildred (Millie) Barlow, b. 1748, d. 1832

Page 65   Elizabeth Barlow, b. 1752, d. 1 Jan 1796; m. John Land, b. ___________, d. 1804. They had nine children. One, named James Land, was born 14 Oct 1792 in KY.

Page 65   Henry Benjamin Barlow Jr, b. 1753, d. 1805; m. Nancy __________. Their issue:

1.   Betsey Walker Barlow, b. ___________, d. ___________; m. in 1814 to Benoni West
2.   Lucinda Barlow, b. ___________, d. ___________; m. in 1815 to William Sutton
3.   Nancy Barlow, b. ___________, d. ___________

4. Mariah Barlow, b. ____________ d. ____________; m. in 1819 to Cussaney Crowder

5. America Lawson Barlow, b. ____________, d. ____________; m. in 1821 to Samuel Crowder

6. Henry A Barlow, b. ____________, d. ____________

7. Odensey Barlow, b. ____________, d. ____________; m. in 1825 to Alexander Kersey

Page 65   Frances Barlow, b. 1755, d. 1 Feb 1849; m. 27 Mar 1792 to Samuel Shepard, b. 1765 in MA. Their issue:

1. William Tompkins Shepard, b. Mar 1793

2. Alphaeus Xavier Francis Shepard, b. Oct 1795

3. Thomas Jefferson Shepard, b. 15 Jan 1801, d. 6 Feb 1875; m. (1) in Nov 1830 to Amanda Smith; they had three children; m. (2) to Mrs Elizabeth Morford (nee Woodruff). They had two children.

4. James Madison Shepard, b. Sep 1802

Page 65   William Barlow, b. 1757, d. 1807; never married

Page 65   William Edward Barlow, b. 18 Sep 1810 in Caroline Co, VA, d. 2 May 1865; m. 23 Dec 1829 to Joanna Seal, b. 20 Dec 1812, d. 25 Feb 1878 of congestive chills in Caroline Co, VA. Their issue:

1. Benjamin Franklin Barlow

2. Mary Jane (Polly) Barlow

3. Sarah K (Sally) Barlow

4. James Lewis Barlow

5. William Henry Barlow

6. John Walter Barlow

7.   Robert D Barlow
8.   Edward Dawson Barlow
9.   Festus S Barlow
10. Edmonia L Barlow
11. Thomas Rosser Barlow

NOTE: For more information on this family, see the book AS I FIND IT, beginning on Page 65.

Page 66   Benjamin Franklin Barlow, b. "30" Sep 1830 in Caroline Co, VA

Page 68   Virginia Anne Puller Blatt, d. 30 Sep 2010; buried in Lakewood Cemetery, Bowling Green, VA

Page 68   Thomas Benjamin Blatt Jr, d. 12 Dec 2005, buried in Lakewood Cemetery, Bowling Green, VA

Page 68   Thomas Benjamin Blatt IV, m. 12 Mar 2004 to Meghan Anne McEvoy. Their issue:

1.   Thomas Benjamin Blatt V, b. 12 Aug 2007
2.   _______________________, b. ___________

Page 68   James Mastin Wigglesworth, b. 16 Oct 1938, d. 12 Nov 1986; buried in Hulls Memorial Cemetery, Falmouth, VA

Page 69   Lucy Frank Allen Dunnington, d. 25 Feb 2010; buried in Lakewood Cemetery, Bowling Green, VA

Page 70   Mark Allen Dunnington, m. (2) 21 Nov 2004 to Tammy Lynette Seymour Garrett, b. 27 Nov 1966. Their issue:

1.   William Levi Dunnington, b. 2 Dec 2003) Twins
2.   Caroline Grace Dunnington, b. 2 Dec 2003)

Page 71   Mary J (Polly)Barlow should read "Mary Jane (Polly) Barlow;
Correction   died 3 May 1916 in Richmond, VA

Page 75   John W Southworth, m. 28 Jan 1903 to Mildred C Doggett. They were married at the bride's home in Caroline Co, VA. John was the son of Mary Jane (Polly) Barlow Southworth and James B Southworth.

Page 77   Issue of John James Pavy III and Anita Carole Knight Pavy:

1.   Miranda Pavy, b. Dec 1999
2.   Evelyn Pavy, b. Feb 2002

Page 78   Lillian Jean Selph, m. Cecil Woodruff Sr. He died 19 Jan 2004 and is buried in High Hills Cemetery, Emporia, VA. Their issue:

1.   Cecil Woodruff Jr
2.   Sherry Jean Woodruff
3.   Shelia Faye Woodruff

Page 78   Sherry Jean Woodruff, m. Richard M Gay. Their issue:
               Christopher M Gay, b. ___________

Page 80   Mary Alice Selph Coker, d. 29 Dec 2007

Page 81   Garnette Ninmo Pavy Waters, d. 9 Apr 2015

Page 81   Issue of John Ryland Pavy and Lori Ann McIntyre Pavy:

                       1.   Ryland Peyton Pavy, b. 5 Jan 2003
                       2.   Rhys Dorian Pavy, b. 15 Sep 2004

Page 82   John Reginald Pavy, d. 3 Feb 2006; buried in Greenlawn Cemetery,
                       Bowling Green, VA

Page 86   Julia Hall Pavy (Pavie), d. 15 Jun 2010; buried in County Line Baptist
                       Church Cemetery, Ruther Glen, VA

Page 87   Francis Chinault Pavy (Pavie), d. 10 Jun 2007; buried in County
                       Line Baptist Church Cemetery, Ruther Glen VA

Page 89   Everett Thomas Pavy's death date should read "3" Dec 1974; buried
Correction   in Maury Cemetery, Richmond, VA

Page 89   Virginia Elizabeth Pavy Hayden, b. 18 Oct 1916, d. 29 Oct 2006;
                       buried in Sunset Memorial Gardens, Fredericksburg, VA

Page 89   William Franklin Perin Jr should read "Franklin William Perin Jr",
Correction   b. 13 Nov 1938, d. 19 Oct 2006; buried in Sunset Memorial Gardens,
                       Fredericksburg, VA

Page 92	Issue of Dallas N Slosjarik and B J O'Bier: Autumn Rivers O'Bier, b. 7 Sep 2006

Page 92	Issue of James Stephen Slosjarik Jr and Kathy Wood:

1. Alexis Faith Slosjarik, b. 26 Mar 2007) Twins
2. Joselyn Grace Slosjarik, b. 26 Mar 2007)

Page 93 Correction	Lois May Pavy Beazley should read Lois "Mae" Pavy Beazley; d. 2 Jul 2015; buried in Washington Memorial Park, Sandston, VA

Page 95	Betty Watson Reed, d. 18 Dec 2005

Page 95	Samuel Alton Reed, m. 20 Feb 2004 to Alice Sweeney Woods, b. 10 Jul 1967

Page 96	Albert I (Hooney) Reed, b. 1937, d. 8 Feb 2005; m. Dyanne __________. He is buried in Schools Family Cemetery, Essex County, VA. Their issue:

1. Jonathan Mark Reed
2. Clay Powell Reed
3. Dawn Reed
4. Dani Reed

Page 97	Edward Hewitt Reed, d. 25 Jan 2005

Page 99   Ryland Hewlett Brooks, d. 26 Jan 2011; buried in Riverside Cemetery, Courtland, VA

Page 99   Christine Gillett should read "Gillette"
Correction

Page 100   Ruth Evelyn Brooks Tomichek , m. (2) Albert G Few Jr

                           Ruth Evelyn Brooks Tomicheck-Few, d. 16 May 2017. She is buried in Manasota Memorial Park, Bradenton, FL

Page 100   Reuben Garnett Brooks, d. 11 Jan 2014; cremated

Page 100   Gloria Hobson Brooks, b. 15 Nov 1932, d. 23 Mar 2013; cremated

Page 101   Thomas David Brooks, d. 29 Jul 2007; buried in Warsaw Baptist Church Cemetery, Warsaw, VA

Page 102   John Chastine Covington, d. 27 Dec 2005

Page 102   Ethel Spencer Covington, d. 24 Nov 2008

Page 103   Caroline Covington Rotella, d. 7 Sep 2008

Page 118   Malcolm Lyle Barlow Jr, m. 3 Apr 1954 to Ann "White"
Correction

Page 121   Helen Parsons Barlow Carver, d. 30 Mar 2006

Page 122   Anna Rosalyn Taylor Landram, d. 4 Apr 2009; buried in Greenlawn
                  Cemetery, Bowling Green, VA

Page 123   Vincent Rudolph Miller, d. 10 Dec 2012; buried in NC

Page 123   Eleanor Taylor Houser, d. 30 Mar 2006; buried in Lakewood Cemetery,
                  Bowling Green, VA

Page 125   Jannelle Anne Wallace should read "Junnelle" Anne Wallace
Correction

Page 125   Issue of Junnelle Anne Wallace and Edward Cleanan Brooks Jr:

                  Edward Cleanan Brooks III, b. 21 Jul 2014

Page 125   Richard Edward (Dickie) Taylor, d. 28 Oct 2006; buried in St. Patrick's
                  Cemetery, Mauston, WI

Page 127   Richard Lewis Barlow; death date should read "6" Jul 1983
Correction

Page 127   Timothy Richard Minner; birth date should read "30 Mar 1973"
Correction

Page 133   Garland Eugene Burnett, d. 23 Jul 2008; buried in Washington
                    Memorial Park Cemetery, Richmond, VA

Page 134   Beatrice Barlow Thomas, d. 30 Dec 2004; buried in Greenlawn
                    Cemetery, Bowling Green, VA

Page 134   John Bradford Thomas' birthdate should read "23" Jul 1976.
Correction

                    Issue of John Bradford Thomas and Regina May Hutchinson, b.
                    1 Apr 1971:

                    Kendall Vaughan Thomas, b. 16 Jul 1996

                    John Bradford Thomas, m. 21 Apr 2001 to Jennifer Songy Waguespack,
                    b. 14 Oct 1976. Their issue:

                    1. Delaney Anne Thomas, b. 23 Jan 2005
                    2. John Alexander Thomas, b. 30 Sep 2008

Page 134   Haley Vaughan Thomas' birthdate should read 18 Mar "1981"
Correction

                    Haley Vaughan Thomas, m. 28 Sep 2002 to Roger Albert Kennedy,
                    b.22 Dec 1977. Their issue:

                    1. Caleb Thomas Kennedy, b. 30 Mar 2003
                    2. Hannah Rae Kennedy, b. 26 Jul 2006
                    3. McKenzie Taylor Kennedy, b. 26 Mar 2008
                    4. Addison Kate Kennedy, b. 19 Apr 2011

Page 135   Brandon Christopher Taylor, m. 27 Sep 2003 to Nancy Elizabeth
Morefield, b. 11 Jul 1976. Their issue:

1.   Catherine Campbell Taylor, b. 1 Dec 2006
2.   Brett Alston Taylor, b. 24 Apr 2009
3.   Kinsey McNeil Taylor, b. 28 Mar 2012

Page 135   Marian Frances Taylor should read "Marion" Frances Taylor.
Correction

Marion Frances Taylor, m. 6 Nov 2004 to Eugene Thomas Mooney,
b. 5 Aug 1974. Their issue:

1.   Megan Faye Mooney, b. 8 Sep 2010
2.   Madison Frances Mooney, b. 15 Oct, 2014

Page 135   Woodford (Woody) Lewis Barlow Jr, d. 2 Nov 2003; buried in
Greenlawn Cemetery, Bowling Green, VA

Page 135   Ruth Allen Barlow, d. 30 Jan 2006; buried in Carmel Church
Cemetery, Ruther Glen, VA

Page 135   Kimberly Lynn Barlow, m. (1) Russell Craig Plotner, b. 23 Jan 1972;
m. (2) Michael Sandy

Page 135   Kristy Lynn Barlow, m. (2) James Morgan McComas, b. 5 May 1975

Page 136   Laura DeBusk should read Laura "Bridgforth" DeBusk, b. 15 Jun 1994

Page 136   Earl Chilton Jr, d. 20 Jun 2016; buried in Lakewood Cemetery, Bowling Green, VA

Page 136   Emily Barlow Chilton, d. 14 Oct 2017; buried in Lakewood Cemetery, Bowling Green, VA

Page 137   Issue of Daniel Collins Webb and Bethany Long Webb:

1.   McKenzie Cason Webb, b. 3 Apr 2000
2.   Jackson Brooks Webb, b. 17 Sep 2003
3.   Emory Spencer Webb, b. 13 Jul 2009

Page 137   Kristin Ann Webb should read Kristin "Anne" Webb.

Page 137   Kristin Anne Webb, m. 10 Mar 2001 to Mark Rajesh Bissoon, b. 5 Sep 1972. Their issue:

1. Ethan Blake Bissoon, b. 12 Jun 2006
2. Ava Dianne Bissoon, b. 14 May 2009
3. Colton Chase Bissoon, b. 21 Dec 2011

Page 137   Chad Lewis Webb, m. 2003 to Emily Grace Sawyer, b. 7 Mar 1980. Their issue:

1.   Weston Lewis Webb, b. 30 Sep 2003
2.   Ella Grace Webb, b. 27 Apr 2006

Page 137   Amanda Leigh Dianis, m. Steven Edward Selph

Page 137   Garnett William Jenkins Jr, b. 2 Nov "1958"

Page 137   Garnett William (Trae) Jenkins III, m. Sabrina ___________. Their issue:

1.   Logan Jenkins, b. ___________
2.   Angel Jenkins, b. 1 Jun 2007, d. 1 Jun 2007

Page 137   Jane Barlow Madison, d. 16 Aug 2012, buried in Lakewood Cemetery, Bowling Green, VA

Page 138   Keith Edward Madison's birthdate should read 26 "July" 1959.
Correction

Page 139   Cordie Gatewood Pitts, d. 13 Apr 2007

Page 139   Ryan Lee Bowie, d. 2 Jan 2005; buried in Hulls Memorial Baptist Church Cemetery, Falmouth, VA

Page 139   Mary Gatewood Pitts, d. 27 Feb 2007

Page 140	Ann E Pitts Hagerty, d. 13 Mar 2015; buried in PA
Page 140	Charles Lewis Hagerty, d. 23 May 2008; buried in PA
Page 140	Donald James Pitts, d. 25 Dec 2015; buried in Salem Baptist Church Cemetery, Sparta, VA

Page 140 — Joshua Dwayne Watts, m. 28 Jun 2000 to Brandy Michelle Perry, b. 9 Feb 1979. Their issue:

1. Courtney Grace Watts, b. 9 Aug 2007) Twins
2. Charles Tucker Watts, b. 9 Aug 2007)

Page 140 — Jared Hugh Watts, m. 8 Dec 2007 to Whitney Sterling Schoonover, b. 28 Jan 1985. Their issue:

1. Kennedy Sterling Watts, b. 26 Mar 2013
2. Reese Aileen Watts, b. 13 Jan 2016
3. Walker Hugh Watts, b. 29 Aug 2018

Page 141
Correction — Burle Daniel (Danny) Trivette's birthdate should read "7" Nov "1962".

Page 141 — Issue of Dawn Pitts Trivette and Burle Daniel (Danny) Trivette:

1. James Austin Trivette, b. 9 Oct 1991
2. Jason Daniel Trivette, b. 17 Jan 1994
3. Jacob Robert Trivette, b. 4 Dec 1995

<table>
<tr><td>Page 141</td><td>Dawn Pitts Trivette, m. (2) 25 May 2011 to Roy A Haun, b. 11 Dec 1971</td></tr>
<tr><td>Page 141</td><td>James Austin Trivette, d. 9 Apr 2013; buried in Salem Baptist Church Cemetery, Sparta, VA</td></tr>
<tr><td>Page 141</td><td>Jennifer Leigh Pitts, d. 18 Jun 2008; buried in PA</td></tr>
<tr><td>Page 141
Correction</td><td>Lenora Skinner Pitts, b. "19 Sep 1916"</td></tr>
<tr><td>Page 144</td><td>Wilbert Lloyd Whittaker Jr, m. (2) 20 May 2009 to Mary Lee Young Pitts, b. 29 Feb 1952</td></tr>
<tr><td>Page 144
Correction</td><td>Wilma Delores Whittaker, m. (1) 1 Aug 1975 to Winston Ernest Haynes, d. "26 Jul 1984". Winston is buried in County Line Baptist Church Cemetery, Ruther Glen, VA.</td></tr>
<tr><td>Page 144</td><td>David Leonard Smith, d. 4 Mar 2002; buried in County Line Baptist Church Cemetery, Ruther Glen</td></tr>
<tr><td>Page 144</td><td>Issue of Wilma Whittaker Smith and David Leonard Smith:

Kendra Faith Smith</td></tr>
</table>

Page 144   Anthony Mark Whittaker, d. 13 May 2005; buried in Mt Vernon Methodist Church Cemetery, Ruther Glen, VA

Page 144   Issue of Dennis Wayne Whittaker and Amy Barlow Whittaker:

Seth Ryan Whittaker, b. 12 Sep 1994 (Adopted 26 Aug 2008)

Page 145   Marcia Pitts Englert, d. 21 Mar 2018 in Richmond, VA; buried in Greenwood Memorial Gardens, Goochland Co, VA

Page 146   Issue of Ardis Burford Fishburne and James Gahan Fishburne Jr:

1.   Catherine Christine Fishburne, b. 12 Jul 2000
2.   James Gahan Fishburne III, b. 18 Sep 2002
3.   Robert Douglas Fishburne, b. 20 Jul 2007

Page 146   John Jason Burford, m. 17 Apr 2004 to Amy Suzanne Harrell. Their issue:

1.   John Thomas Burford, b. 24 Feb 2009 in Richmond, VA
2.   Caroline Batson Burford, b. 15 Apr 2011 in Richmond, VA

Page 146
Correction   Joycelyn Hilton Pitts should read "Jocelyn".

Page 146   Jocelyn Hilton Pitts, m. 10 Oct 2010 to Gary John Lowzik Jr, b. 10 Feb 1979. Their issue:

Emily Alexis Lowzik, b. 4 Nov 2018 in Richmond, VA

Page 147   Sarah Almeda Pitts, m. 11 Aug 2007 to Ryan Colvin. Their issue:

1. Randolph Barrett (Rett) Colvin, b. 31 Jul 2011
2. Ryland Bruce (Riley) Colvin, b. 25 Aug 2013
3. Caroline Elizabeth Colvin, b. 26 Aug 2016
4. Robert Burton (Robbie) Colvin, b. 5 Apr 2018

Page 147   Anne Elizabeth Pitts, m. 9 Sep 2006 to Jacob Landon Grove. Their issue:

1. Charlotte Anne Grove, b. 16 Apr 2012
2. Jack Randolph Grove, b. 10 Oct 2014

Page 147   Jennifer Carol Pitts, m. 22 Oct 2016 to Matthew Scott Anns, b. 16 Apr 1987. Her issue:

Adam James Pitts, b. 31 Jan 2006

Their issue:

Lily Grace Anns, b. 23 Apr 2018

Page 147   Christopher Nelson Pitts, m. 2 May 2015 to Laura Owens, b. 24 Oct 1988. Their issue:

1. Levi Owen Pitts, b. 10 Jan 2017
2. Caleb Nelson Pitts, b. 27 Sep 2018

Page 147   David Sterling Ganoe Jr, d. 17 Nov 2006; buried in Salem Baptist Church Cemetery, Sparta, VA

Page 154   Margaret Denson Young, d. 30 Jan 2005

Page 160   Phillip Woodford Satterwhite, d. 27 Nov 2018; buried in Greenlawn
                  Cemetery, Bowling Green, VA

Page 160   Aubrey Franklin Satterwhite, d. 29 Jul 2006; buried in Greenlawn
                  Cemetery, Bowling Green, VA

Page 160   Andrew Thomas Satterwhite, m. 5 Nov 2011 to Kendall Ryan Barlow,
                  b. 11 Sep 1989. Their issue:

                  Savannah Ryan Satterwhite, b. 27 Aug 2017

Page 161   Michael Wayne Satterwhite, m. (2) 25 May 2002 to Gloria Jean
                  Ryals, b. 28 Jun 1949

Page 161   Michael Wayne Satterwhite, d. 25 Oct 2016; buried in Greenlawn
                  Cemetery, Bowling Green, VA

Page 161   Kellam Fred Brooks, d. 28 Feb 2014; buried in Greenlawn Cemetery,
                  Bowling Green, VA

Page 161   Issue of Ethel Lynn Brooks Sale and James Russell Sale:

                  1. Logan Ashley Sale, b. 1 Dec 1996
                  2. Shelby Sale, b. ___________

Page 161 Correction	Percy Franklin Satterwhite Jr's birthdate should read 18 Nov "1949".
Page 161	Percy Franklin Satterwhite Jr, d. 7 Nov 2010; buried in Greenlawn Cemetery, Bowling Green, VA
Page 162	William Alexander Ayers, b. 9 Sep 2004 in Fredericksburg, VA
Page 163	Lena Bradley Brooks Clore, d. 25 Aug 2003; buried in Zoan Baptist Church Cemetery, Spotsylvania, VA
Page 165	Lottie Lillian (Bill) Brooks, d. 11 Aug 2006
Page 166	Adel Barlow Warren, d. 23 Nov 2003; buried in Liberty Baptist Church Cemetery, Appomattox, VA
Page 167	Ruby Puller Barlow, d. 18 Oct 2005
Page 167	Warren Eugene Barlow, d. 15 Dec 2018; buried in Signal Hill Memorial Park, Hanover, VA
Page 167	Nancy Toombs Barlow, d. 17 Sep 2008; buried in Signal Hill Memorial Park, Hanover, VA

Page 168   Paul Weston Barlow, d. 22 Jul 2011

Page 168   Irene Southworth Young, d. 18 May 2005

Page 172   Issue of Pearl Barlow Mitchell and Curtis Mitchell:

                  Unnamed Son, b. 2 Jan 1936, d. 2 Jan 1936

Page 173   Lucy Barlow Bullock, d .17 Jan 2006

Page 175   Charles Tate Brown, m. 7 Nov 1998 to Jennie Marie Wray, b. 24
                  Mar 1981

Page 175   Roger Lee Taylor Sr, d. 24 Apr 2009; buried in Signal Hill Memorial
                  Park, Hanover VA

Page 176   Charles Boyd Mitchell Sr, d. 14 Oct 2006; buried in Signal Hill
                  Memorial Park, Hanover, VA

Page 176   Catherine Barlow Mitchell, d. 2 Feb 2015; buried in Signal Hill
                  Memorial Park, Hanover, VA

Page 177   Neil Dexter Wood should read "Neal" Dexter Wood
Correction

Page 181   Ann Marie Carter Bristow, d. 1 May 2014

Page 182   Faye Emery Carter, d. 14 Mar 2007; buried in Glebe Landing Baptist
                  Church, Middlesex Co, VA

Page 182   Harry Osborne Bullock, d. 8 Sep 2008; husband of Dorothy Barlow
                  Street Bullock

Page 183   Lewis Walter Barlow Jr, d. 28 Apr 2008; buried in Concord Baptist
                  Church Cemetery, Ruther Glen, VA

Page 183   Verna Mitchell Barlow, d. 24 Nov 2017; buried in Concord Baptist
                  Church Cemetery, Ruther Glen, VA

Page 183   Hope Barlow Gatewood, m. (2) 9 Jan 2016 to Donald Alan Clark, b.
                  9 Mar 1944

Page 184   Hailey Elizabeth Reid's birthdate should read "5 Jun 2000".

Page 184   Issue of Stacy Lynn Gatewood and Richard Tyler McGrath:

                  1.   Juliana Hope McGrath, b. 27 Jun 2001
                  2.   Kelsey Elizabeth McGrath, b. 1 Feb 2003
                  3.   Richard Kenneth Tyler McGrath, b. 13 Apr 2005

Page 184   Heather Lee Gordon, m. Robert Lawson. Their issue:

                  1.   Afton Elias Lawson, b. 3 Jul 2009
                  2.   Rowan C Lawson, b. 28 Feb 2011

Page 185	Issue of Jason Clay Barlow and Taryn Rice Barlow:
	Micah Clay Barlow, b. 25 Apr 2010

Page 185 Correction	Carolyn Ann Barlow, m. 28 Nov 1970 to (1) Emerson Monroe Gray "Jr".

Page 185   Tracey Kathleen Gray, m. 20 Sep 2003 to Ashley Philip Mallory, b. 13 Aug 1975. Their issue:

1. Nolan Ashley Mallory, b. 26 Aug 2007 in Mechanicsville, VA
2. Emerson Kathleen Mallory, b. 5 Feb 2011 in Mechanicsville, VA

Page 185 Correction   Ashley Barlow Gray's birthdate should read 4 Sep "1979".

Page 185   Ashley Barlow Gray, m. 21 Feb 2007 to Cathy Jo Wright. Their issue:

1. Kailey Alexis Gray, b. 3 Oct 2000 in Fredericksburg, VA
2. Kamryn Ashley Gray, b. 4 Sep 2003 in Fredericksburg, VA

Page 186   Catherine Barlow Myers, m. (2) 25 Apr 2009 to Clarence James Pitts, b. 10 Apr 1946

Page 186   Daniel Ray Myers, m. 12 Oct 2013 to Stacy Lynn Fox, b. 18 Jan 1985.

Their issue:

Colton Ray Myers, b. 27 Aug 2015

Page 186   Alison Elizabeth Myers, m. 23 Jun 2018 to David Tyler Floyd, b. 18 Mar 1989. Her issue:

Chelsea Lee Shiflett, b. 7 Jul 2011 in Mechanicsville, VA

Page 186   Matthew Wayne Johnson, m. (2) 23 Jun 2007 to Stephanie Ann Jessie, b. 11 Sep 1985. Their issue:

1. Deacon Luke Johnson, b. 16 Jan 2008 in Mechanicsville, VA
2. Ezra Holden Johnson, b. 4 Aug 2016 in Mechanicsville, VA

Page 186   Issue of Amy Barlow Whittaker and Dennis Wayne Whittaker:

Seth Ryan Whittaker, b. 12 Sep 1994 (Adopted 26 Aug 2008)

Page 186   Demple Chenault Barlow, d. 14 Jun 2008; buried in Concord Baptist Church Cemetery, Ruther Glen, VA

Page 186   Patricia Clarke Barlow, b. 8 Apr 1964, d. 13 Feb 2012; buried in Concord Baptist Church Cemetery, Ruther Glen, VA

Page 186   Kendall Ryan Barlow, m. 5 Nov 2011 to Andrew Thomas Satterwhite, b. 12 Jan 1989. Their issue:

Savannah Ryan Satterwhite, b. 27 Aug 2017

Page 187   Issue of Kristina Marie Barlow:

1.   Tyra Marie Barlow should read Tyra Marie "Brown", b. 17 Feb 2000, d. 20 Mar 2016; buried in Concord Baptist Church Cemetery, Ruther Glen, VA
2.   Kamal Joran Justice
3.   Nakyah Yanal Justice

Page 187   Kenneth Lee Utz, d. 29 Jul 2015; buried in Virginia Veterans Cemetery, Amelia, VA

Page 187   Issue of Kenneth Lamont Utz and Constance Bowman Utz:

1.   Emily Jean Utz, b. 14 Oct 1993
2.   Katherine Elizabeth Utz, b. 21 Sep 1997

Page 187   Issue of Ronald Scott Utz and Loretta Easterling Utz:

1.   Fallon Nicole Utz, b. 5 Sep 1991; m. Brandon Osborne
2.   Austin Michael Utz, b. 18 Feb 1993
3.   Dalton Gray Utz, b. 21 Mar 1996

Page 187   Shirley Barlow Minter, d. 4 Jun 2013; buried in Powhatan Community Cemetery, Powhatan Co, VA

Page 188   Issue of Roger Dean Minter and Tessa Umbarger Minter:

1. Evan Asher Minter, b. 12 May 1989
2. Lindsey Michelle Minter, b. 24 Nov 1992
3. Ryan Minter, b. ___________

Issue of Lindsey Michelle Minter:

Dylan ___________, b. 5 Apr 2017

Page 188   Elizabeth Barlow Brawner Reynolds, d. 12 Jan 2005; Guy Rush Reynolds, d. 1 Sep 2009

Page 191   Laura Abel Barlow, d. 25 Jan 2010; buried in Dumfries Cemetery, Dumfries, VA. Her husband, Melvin Lloyd Barlow Jr. is also buried there.

Page 191   Donald Wray Lewis, d. 17 Feb 2012

Page 191   Virginia Barlow Rohs, d. Dec 2010; buried in Quantico National Cemetery

Page 191   John Rohs Jr., d. 10 May 1999; buried in Quantico National Cemetery

Page 192   Marie Barlow Woodle, d. 20 Mar 2008; buried in Westhampton Memorial Park, Richmond, VA

Page 192	John Wesley Woodle Sr, d. 19 Jul 2019; buried in Westhampton Memorial Park, Richmond, VA
Page 195	Ennis Bradford Barlow, d. 26 Jul 2010; buried in Fairview Memorial Gardens, Stockbridge,GA
Page 195	Betty Cook Barlow, d. 19 Mar 2009; buried in Fairview Memorial Gardens, Stockbridge, GA
Page 196	Elaine Barlow Cramme', d. 19 Jun 2015; buried in Concord Baptist Church Cemetery, Ruther Glen, VA
Page 196	Joseph Wilbur Harver Jr, d. 11 Nov 2003; buried in Virginia Veterans Cemetery, Amelia, VA
Page 197	Micah Hughes Royall, d. 6 Sep 2009; buried in Sandy Creek Baptist Church Cemetery, Amelia Co, VA
Page 197	Ralph Linwood Barlow, d. 15 Oct 2010; cremated and to be buried at a later date in Sacramento Valley National Cemetery, Dixon, CA
Page 197 Correction	Billie Lucietta Morgan Barlow's middle name should read "Lucetta"

Page 197   Aaron Christopher Nathan's middle name should read "Kristofer"
Correction

Page 197   Issue of Erich Kevin Nathan and Nicole Baker Nathan:

                  William Isaiak Nathan, b. 28 Aug 2007

Page 197   Donavan Alan Barlow, b. 14 Sep 2003

Page 197   Issue of Joshua Wayne Woo and wife:

                  1.   Josephine Alison Woo, b. 9 Jul 2016
                  2.   Isabel Caroline Woo, b. 11 Jun 2018

Page 198   James Michael Barlow, m. 24 Jul 2004 to Whitney Leigh Vanschoonhoven,
                  b. 1 Jul 1985

Page 198   Katie Sue Barlow, m. 2 Sep 2018 to Tony Dwire

Page 198   Angeleigh Kaydon Barlow, b. 5 May 2005

Page 198   Elsie Barlow Harmon, d. 1 Feb 2013

Page 198   Elwood Baker Harmon, d. 15 May 2008

Page 198   Issue of Susan Harmon Epperson and Thomas Davies Epperson:

             Alexander Christian Epperson, b. 25 Aug 2004

Page 199   James Ray Waddill, d. 20 Jul 2007; buried in Concord Baptist Church
             Cemetery, Ruther Glen, VA

Page 199   Robert D Barlow, b. Mar 1843 in Caroline Co, VA, d. c. 1925 in
             Richmond, VA; m. 11 Dec 1867 to Bettie L Dunn, b. 1850, d. 1898.

             Their issue:

             1.   Joseph E Barlow
             2.   Unnamed Child
             3.   Charles M Barlow
             4.   Robert Samuel Barlow
             5.   Andrew Dunn Barlow
             6.   Sallie Kate Barlow
             7.   Lenny Barlow
             8.   Alice Wilbur Barlow

Page 202   Joseph E Barlow, b. 1872, d. Jul 1873 in Caroline Co, VA

             Unnamed Child, b. 16 Sep 1868; d. 1868 in Caroline Co, VA

             Charles M Barlow, b. 1 Sep 1869, d. 21 Jun 1923; m. 1896 to
             Emma Sauvager, b. 28 Apr 1872, d. 29 Sep 1939. Their issue:

             1.   Mary Rebecca Barlow, b. 1897 in Caroline Co, VA; m. 16 Mar
                  1914 in Richmond, VA to Charles L Gullett Jr, b. ___________

2. George Pearman Barlow, b. 29 Aug 1898 in Caroline Co, VA, d. 1936

3. Alice F Barlow, b. 1902

4. Willie G Barlow, b. 1903

5. Mattie S Barlow, b. 1905

6. James H Barlow, b. 1908

Page 202   Robert Samuel Barlow, b. 19 Jul 1875 in Caroline Co, VA, d. __________; m. 7 Aug 1909 to Buford Gravely, b. 1886

Page 202   Andrew Dunn Barlow, Pipefitter, b. 23 Nov 1881 in Caroline Co, VA, d. 10 Nov 1949 in Richmond, VA, of carcinoma of the esophagus; m. 24 Jan 1906 to Ida Carneal. He is buried in Gethsemane Christian Church Cemetery in Hanover Co, VA

Page 202   Sallie Kate Barlow, b. 5 Feb 1885 in Caroline Co, VA, d. 30 Oct 1908 in Richmond, VA. She is buried in Oakwood Cemetery, Richmond, VA

Page 202   Lenny Barlow, b. Jun 1887, d. 20 Aug 1887 at "Arnolds Hill' in Caroline Co, VA

Page 202   Alice Wilbur Barlow, b. 28 Apr 1890 in Caroline Co, VA, d. 27 Jan 1978 of heart disease in Somerset (Orange Co), VA; m. Leonard G Shipp (Opechancanough Tribe #118—IMP O.R.M.), b. 1 Apr 1892, d. 24 Jun 1934. They are buried in the Shipp Family Cemetery, Barboursville, VA. Their issue:

1. Waverly I Shipp, b. 1917

2. George R Shipp, b. 1919

3. Leonard G Shipp Jr, b. 1923

Page 216   Kenneth Stephen Stewart Jr, m. 1 Nov 2004 to Susan Elizabeth
                   Guess, b. 4 Apr 1976. Their issue:

                   1. Kaylie Elizabeth Stewart, b. 7 Mar 2006
                   2. Madison Ann Stewart, b. 2 Dec 2008

Page 216   Joseph Wade Burton's birth date should read "13 Jun 1973"
Correction

Page 216   Issue of Jamie Wray Farmer Burton and Joseph Wade Burton:

                   1. Josie Wray Burton, b. 30 Sep 2007
                   2. Cayden James Burton, b. 3 Jun 2010)   Twins
                   3. Carter Joseph Burton, b. 3 Jun 2010)

Page 216   Meredith Ryan Lane Carter's birthdate should read "25" Apr "1977".
Correction

Page 216   Issue of William Maynard Carter III and Meredith Ryan Lane Carter:

                   1. William Maynard Carter IV, b. 23 Feb 2005
                   2. Harrison Lane Carter, b. 3 May 2007
                   3. Graham Patrick Carter, b. 16 Sep 2011
                   4. Mary Katherine Spencer Carter, b. 1 Mar 2017

Page 216   Jennifer Meade Carter, m. (2) 13 May 2008 to Chip Hartle. Issue
                   by second marriage:

                   1. Ella Grace Hartle, b. 14 May 2009
                   2. Kaelynn Hope Hartle, b. 26 Mar 2012

Page 216	Scott Tyler Pitts, m. Jennifer __________. Their issue: Kieran Ryan Pitts, b. 16 Mar 2010
Page 219	Letty Mills Crisp, d. 11 Feb 2004
Page 222	Jane Barlow Madison, d. 16 Aug 2012, buried in Lakewood Cemetery, Bowling Green, VA
Page 222 Correction	Keith Edward Madison's birthdate should read 26 "July" 1959.
Page 223	Jeffrey Allen Taylor, d. 19 Oct 2018
Page 224	Frances Taylor Wendt, d. 31 May 2005; buried in Middletown, OH
Page 224	Dale Edward Wendt, d. 24 Jun 2003; buried in Middletown, OH
Page 224	Michael Clift Hardin, d. 1 Mar 2009; buried in Trinity United Methodist Church Cemetery, King George, VA
Page 225	Manley Dillard Taylor, d. 4 Oct 2016; buried Lakewood Cemetery, Bowling Green, VA

Page 225   Lois Covington Taylor, d. 12 Sep 2009; buried Lakewood Cemetery, Bowling Green, VA

Page 225   Manley Dillard Taylor Jr, d. 20 Jan 2004

Page 225   Leah Michelle Taylor, m. 11 Oct 2008 to Russell Brian Acors. Their issue:

                Jordan Acors, b. ___________

Page 225   Kristen Denise Taylor, m. 6 Jun 2009 to Ian Christopher Kraynak

Page 226   Joyce Pitts Wilson, d. 16 Apr 2018; buried in County Line Baptist Church Cemetery, Ruther Glen, VA

Page 226   Robin Elizabeth Wilson, d. 19 May 1970. She was moved from Central Baptist Church Cemetery, Richmond, VA, to County Line Baptist Church Cemetery, Ruther Glen, VA.

Page 227   Issue of Susan Wilson Morley and Peter Kevin Morley:

                1. Peter Kieran Morley, b. 24 Oct 2002
                2. Caroline Meredith Morley, b. 2 Sep 2004

Page 227   Marion Joyce Kelley Baughan, d. 17 Dec 2014; buried in St. Stephen's Church Cemetery, St Stephen's Church, VA

Page 227
Correction

Kelly Sue Baughan should read "Kelley"

Page 228

Issue of Cara Dunnavant Alexander and Justin Eugene Alexander:

Ainsley Elizabeth Alexander, b. 22 Jun 2004, Richmond, VA

Page 228
Correction

Neale Wayne Kelley's birth date should read 10 May "1949". Neale Wayne Kelley, d. 25 Jun 2017; cremated

Page 228

Jacquelin Pleasants Kelley, d. 8 Nov 2014

Page 229

William Edward Watts, d. 12 May 2004; buried in Vauter's Episcopal Church Cemetery, Loretto, VA

Page 229

Stephanie Ryan Covington, m. (2) 4 Apr 2015 to Benjamin Jeffrey-Preece Sadler, b. 2 Nov 1987

Page 229

Karla Renee Covington, m. 12 May 2018 to Ryan Perry Eutsler, b. 30 Jul 1985

Page 229

Courtney Liane Covington, m. 27 Oct 2012 to James Jeremy Taylor, b. 2 Dec 1982. Their issue:

Sophia Mae Taylor, b. 14 Jul 2019

Page 230   Issue of Krysta Lynn Gill and Jonathan Art Jackson:

Jocelyn Avery Jackson, b. 15 Dec 2013

Page 230   Issue of Meagan Renee Gill and Ashley Kyle Beamon:

Bryce Mason Beamon, b. 18 Sep 2014

Page 230   Andrew Michael Gill, m. 15 Oct 2005 to Christy Michelle Warren, b. 22 Mar 1976. Their issue:

1.   Taylor Lee-Anne Gill, b. 6 Aug 2003
2.   Peyton Sue Gill, b. 17 May 2008

Page 230   Robert Carroll Beazley III, m. 18 Oct 2008 to Valerie Basoco. Their issue:

1.   Robert Carroll Beazley IV, b. 3 Jan 2009 in CA
2.   Summer Valentina Beazley, b. 19 Aug 2010 in CA

Page 231   Mark Alan Beazley, m. 9 May 2009 to Amber Nicole Link. Their issue:

Delaney Lynn Beazley, b. 1 Mar 2010 in Newport News, VA

Page 231   Issue of Johanna Elizabeth Beazley:

Bailey Elizabeth Tilley, b. 29 Jul 2009

Page 231	Lillian Pitts Pugh Pavy, d. 29 Nov 2016; buried in Mt Hermon Baptist Church Cemetery, Shumansville, VA
Page 231	Robert Woodford (Dick) Pitts, d. 29 May 2018; buried in Mt Hermon Baptist Church Cemetery, Shumansville, VA
Page 232	Issue of Taylor Madeline Roberts:
	Karson Deaton, b. 26 Dec 2013
Page 232	Issue of Christopher Lanny Fulford and Crystal Wilder Fulford:
	Chase Wyatt Fulford, b. 17 Jun 2007
Page 232	Katherine Louise Phillips, m. 20 Jun 2015 to Chad Devine, b. __________
	Issue of Katherine (Katie) Phillips Devine and Bryan Marzo:
	Everly Katherine Marzo, b. 8 Feb 2019
Page 233 Correction	James Joseph Hartman should read "Joseph James" Hartman
Page 233	Joseph James Hartman, d. 15 Dec 2006; buried in Holy Cross Cemetery, Cleveland, OH
Page 233	Ian James McHugh, m. (1) 19 Aug 2008 to Tami H Brown; m (2)

20 Jul 2018 to Betsy Woods Lenahan, b. 25 May 1979. Issue by first marriage:

Neala Dolly McHugh, b. 8 Dec 2014 in CA

Page 233   Nellie Ann McHugh, m. 15 Jul 2017 to Tyler Wade Tingley, b. 30 Sep 1977. Their issue:

Owen Ronald Tingley, b. 17 May 2018

Page 233   John David Hartman, m. (2) 12 Oct 2002 to Michelle Louise Hornbach, b. 4 Mar 1971. Their issue:

1.   John Carter (Jack) Hartman, b. 31 Jul 2006 in Chicago, IL
2.   Henry Joseph Hartman, b. 22 Oct 2009 in Chicago, IL

Page 233   Edward Dawson Pitts, d. 26 Nov 2011; cremated

Page 234   Mabel Pitts Weymouth, d. 1 Oct 2018; buried in Mt Hermon Baptist Church Cemetery, Shumansville, VA

Page 234   Julian Roy (Big Boy) Carter Sr, d. 13 Dec 2018; buried in Greenlawn Cemetery, Bowling Green, VA

Page 234   Lisa Kay Carter Burch, m. (2) 21 Nov 2009 to John Woodroof. Issue by second marriage:

Julianne Isabella Woodroof, b. 1 Feb 2011

Page 234   Benny Sale Brooks, d. 1 Sep 2016; cremated

Page 235   Jonathan Benjamin Brooks, m. 4 Jun 2016 to Lauren Elizabeth
                  Didlake, b. 23 Sep 1991. Their issue:

                  Carter Elizabeth Brooks, b. 9 May 2017 in Richmond, VA

Page 235   Irene Zicafoose Pitts, d. 2 Feb 2011; buried in Mt Hermon Baptist
                  Church Cemetery, Shumansville, VA

Page 235   John Eric Oakes, m. 21 Jun 2003 to Kellie Gardner. Their issue:

                  1.   Everett Liam Gardner Oakes, b. 15 Mar 2013 in ME
                  2.   Fianna Elsie Anadalyn Oakes, b. 12 Nov 2015 in ME

Page 235   Michael Brandon Oakes, born in Maine should read born in
Correction   "Portsmouth, VA"

Page 235   Michael Brandon Oakes, m. 31 Oct 2008 to Rachel Feero, b. 24 Mar
                  1981. Their issue:

                  1.   Oscar Malcolm Eastwood Oakes, b. 19 Feb 2008 in ME
                  2.   Emerson Enzo Feero Oakes, b. 8 Apr 2010 in ME
                  3.   Tesla River Violet Oakes, b. 9 Apr 2015 in ME

Page 235   Katie Lea Oakes, m. 26 Jul 2008 to Conor McMahon, b. 15 Aug 1978.
                  Their issue:

1.   Virginia June Oakes McMahon, b. 14 Oct 2009 in NM
2.   Cassius Owen Oakes McMahon, b. 29 Jan 2012 in KY

Page 235   Scott Andrew Oakes, m. Dora Bowden. Their Issue:

1.   Kolee Mae Oakes, b. 13 Nov 2002 in Waterville, ME
2.   Brandon Zane Oakes, b. 18 Nov 2006 in Waterville, ME

Issue of Scott Andrew Oakes and Shannon Marie Alexander:

Landon Roger Alexander, b. 2 Jul 2009

Issue of Scott Andrew Oakes and Twanic Poliquin:

Alexiyah Poliquin, b. 24 Aug 2011 in ME

Page 235   Rebecca Lynn Oakes, m. 5 Nov 2011 to Timothy Dean DeWitt, b.
9 Jun 1981. Their issue:

1.   Hannah Lea Oakes, b. 29 Jul 2006 in ME
2.   Norah Elizabeth Oakes, b. 7 Oct 2010
3.   Carter Dean DeWitt, b. 30 Apr 2012

Page 235   Sarah Elizabeth Edwards, m. 25 May 2013 to Stephen Michael
Salvato. Their issue:

1.   Lillian Elizabeth Salvato, b. 3 Jul 2014 in Richmond, VA
2.   Eleanor Catherine Salvato, b. 6 Mar 2019 born in Rich-
     mond, VA

Page 236   Issue of Charles Russell Dalton and Jennifer Nicole Champion, b. 16 Apr 1985:

Brandon Scott Champion-Dalton, b. 7 May 2004

Page 236   Issue of Charles Russell Dalton and Holly Coleman:

Annabelle Hope Dalton, b. 9 Jan 2017

Page 236   Melanie Laverne Pitts Church, m. (2) 11 Aug 2007 to Eric Allen Wilson

Page 236   Kristina Marie Church, m. 14 Nov 2015 to Christopher Wyatt Robens, b. 31 Aug 1989. Their issue:

1. Nolan Weston Robens, b. 26 Jul 2013
2. Ethan Colton Robens, b. 8 Nov 2016

Page 237   Dawn Aniello Pitts, d. 25 Dec 2017; cremated

Page 237   Thomas Lee Pitts III, m. Jessica Mondajar. Their issue:

1. Addison Jean Pitts, b. 3 Feb 2017 in Richmond, VA
2. Raylyne Marie Pitts, b. 23 Oct 2018 in Richmond, VA

Page 237   Rae Covington Gatewood, d. 22 Jun 2014

Page 237   Jeanne Gatewood Clapp, d. 5 Jun 2014; buried in MD

Page 237   Roger Carlton Gatewood, d. 16 Jun 2015 in Austin, TX; buried in
                  St Pauline's Cemetery, Windsor, ND

Page 239   Atwell Burruss (Nick) Byrd, m. Carrie Anne McKinney: Their issue:

                  1.   Kylie MacKenzie Byrd, b. 11 Oct 2008
                  2.   Shane Hunter Byrd, b. 24 Jul 2014

Page 239   Elizabeth Taylor Wallace, d. Apr 2015; buried in Arlington National
                  Cemetery

Page 240   Anna Rosalyn Taylor Landram, d. 4 Apr 2009; buried in Greenlawn
                  Cemetery, Bowling Green, VA

Page 240   Vincent Rudolph Miller, d. 10 Dec 2012; buried in NC

Page 240   Eleanor Taylor Houser, d. 30 Mar 2006; buried in Lakewood Cemetery,
                  Bowling Green, VA

Page 241   Jannelle Anne Wallace should read "Junnelle" Anne Wallace
Correction

Page 241   Issue of Junnelle Anne Wallace and Edward Cleanan Brooks Jr:
                  Edward Cleanan Brooks III, b. 21 Jul 2014

Page 248   Adam Thomas Carnegie, m. 29 Nov 2008 to Karen (Kacey) Robbins: Their issue:

Ellison Carol Carnegie, b. 4 Mar 2014 in Norfolk, VA

Page 248   Alice Carroll Carnegie, m. David Paul Harris. Their issue:

1.   Easton Taylor Harris, b. 28 Mar 2013 in Suffolk, VA
2.   Blake Lambert Harris, b. 29 Aug 2017 in Suffolk, VA

Page 248   Aaron William Carnegie, m. Sandra Collick. Their issue:

Bryce William Carnegie, b. 20 Oct 2012 in Suffolk, VA

Page 248   Carroll Lawrence (Billy) Pitts, d. 29 May 2010; buried in Mt Hermon Baptist Church Cemetery, Shumansville, VA

Page 249   Lelia Floyd Pitts Loving, d. 19 Sep 2008; buried in Mt Hermon Baptist Church Cemetery, Shumansville, VA

Page 250   Joseph Alexander Barlow Jr, d. 5 Mar 2012; buried in Mt Hermon Baptist Church Cemetery, Shumansville, VA

Page 250   Ruby Whittaker Barlow, d. 20 Sep 2004; buried in Mt Hermon Baptist Church Cemetery, Shumansville, VA

Page 251   Mellissa Lynn Barlow, m. Charles Ryan Morrell. Their issue:

                 Addison Lee Morrell, b. 6 Mar 2009

Page 251   Edward Michael Truslow, d. 5 Sep 2005; buried in Mt Hermon
                 Baptist Church Cemetery, Shumansville, VA

Page 251   Edwin Grieg Barlow, m. (2) 2 Aug 2008, Kathrine Anne Stoneman

Page 251   William Edward Barlow, d. 23 Nov 2015; buried Mt Hermon Baptist
                 Church Cemetery, Shumansville, VA

Page 251   Irene Cooper Barlow, d. 9 Oct 2009; buried Mt Hermon Baptist
                 Church Cemetery, Shumansville, VA

Page 252   Jason Ryan Houston, m. (1) 22 Jun 2002 to Angela Kay Southworth,
                 b. 10 Dec 1977; m. (2) 10 Sep 2011 to Rebecca Amy Jackson.

Page 252   Ashley Barlow Gray's birthdate should read 4 Sep "1979."

Page 252   Cathy Jo Wright, m. 21 Feb 2007 to Ashley Barlow Gray. Their issue:

                 1. Kailey Alexis Gray, b. 3 Oct 2000 in Fredericksburg, VA
                 2. Kamryn Ashley Gray, b. 4 Sep 2003 in Fredericksburg, VA

Page 253   Bezaleel Brown Landes' death date should read "11 Mar 1953".
Correction

Page 253   Laura Belle (Lottie) Barlow Armstrong, d. 26 Nov 2009; buried in
                  Forest Lawn Cemetery, Richmond, VA

Page 253   Nancy Sue Harrelson Walton, d. 19 Jan 2015

Page 253   Welford Arlen Reece Jr, d. 16 Oct 2010; buried in Mt Hermon
                  Baptist Church Cemetery, Shumansville, VA

Page 254   Gussie Barlow Taylor, d. 3 Dec 2018; buried in Forest Lawn Cemetery,
                  Richmond, VA

Page 256   Raymond Arthur (Chip) Lamont, d. 27 May 2018; buried in NM

Page 256   Anna Bryant Barlow, d. 10 Mar 2007; buried in Mt Hermon Baptist
                  Church Cemetery, Shumansville, VA

Page 256   Lester Bryant Barlow, d. 14 Aug 2012; buried in Mt Hermon Baptist
                  Church Cemetery, Shumansville, VA

Page 260   Beatrice Irene Barlow Barchet, d. 25 Oct 2008; buried in Forest
                  Lawn Cemetery, Richmond, VA

THE BARLOW CASE.

Street-Car Men's Union Consider His Discharge by Traction Company.

The Street Railway Employes' Union held a long meeting last night from 8 o'clock until nearly midnight, the larger part of which was given to the consideration of the discharge by the Traction Company of Motorman Robert Barlow, the vice-president of the union.

No final action was taken. A committee has had the matter in hand and will probably continue negotiations and report to a later meeting. When seen after the meeting Mr. Barlow preferred not to make a statement for the press just yet. President Simmons also thought the time had not come for the union to publicly discuss the matter.

The men think Barlow has been treated badly, but they are not looking for trouble and hope the company may see its way clear to some settlement of the affair satisfactory to all parties.

Barlow was discharged, it is reported, because of his having made some objection to an alleged order of the dispatcher to fall back or run ahead as much as two minutes on Main Street at discretion.

This Barlow objected to, as he interpreted it to indicate a desire to hold back and catch the travel of the cars of the other company on Main Street. There has been some complaint that Traction cars sometimes creep along on Main Street as though to retard the other company.

President Remiss, of the Traction Company, states that no order to hold back the cars of the other company has been issued, and that Barlow was discharged for insubordination.

"The Barlow Case"

Pleasant Birthday Party.

An attractive birthday party was given at the residence of Mr. R. D. Barlow, No. 305 North Eighteenth Street, Tuesday night, in honor of the sixteenth birthday of his daughter Kate.

Games, music and dancing were indulged in until an early hour in the morning.

Those present were Mrs. Jennie Butler, Mrs. Annie Barlow, Mrs. Lillian Barlow, Misses Blanch Jeter, Hattie Jeter, Ida Carneal, Bertie Carneal, Ethel Chiles, Anna Loving, Willie Sirles, Daisy Sirles, Mollie Pool, Annie Batton, Florence Reams, Kate Barlow, Alice Barlow, Emma Vaughan, Lula Walker, Messrs. Lem Butler, George Butler, Andrew Barlow, R. S. Barlow, Archie Stuart, Leonard Loving, Willie Jeter, Marshall Reams, Vivian Reams, Lewis Miller, of Baltimore; Johnnie Sirles, Charlie Overby, Fred Treewiller, Richard Longest, Sam Jones, Emmet Martin and Frank Shaw.

Pleasant Birhday Party newspaper clipping.

APPLICATION FOR MEMBERSHIP
ISSUED BY AUTHORITY OF THE NATIONAL BOARD OF TRUSTEES

TO THE BOARD OF MANAGERS OF

THE District of Columbia SOCIETY
OF THE
NATIONAL SOCIETY
SONS OF THE AMERICAN REVOLUTION

I, Thurston E. Baxter, being of the age of 45 years hereby apply for membership in this Society by right of lineal descent in the following line from

Thomas Barlow II

who was born in Virginia on the 25th day of Aug, 17 60 and died in Kentucky on the 30th day of Jan, 825

and who assisted in establishing American Independence.

I was born in Jerseyville, County of Jersey State of Illinois on the 12th day of May 1905.

(1) I am the son of Leslie I. Baxter born 3/2/1877, died 10/8/1942, and his wife Ida Ann Heldersheid born 12/19/1870, died 7/12/1929, married 1/20/1892

(2) grandson of Squire John Baxter born 8/7/1839, died 12/2/1911, and his wife Amanda Jane Barlow born 5/11/1841, died 11/2/1929, married 4/21/1897

(3) great-grandson of Martin B. Barlow born 11/1/1802, died 8/21/1871, and his wife Elizabeth Searing born 6/21/1816, died 2/27/1852, married 10/17/1836

(4) great-grandson of Thomas Barlow II born 8/25/1760, died 1/30/1825, and his wife Susan Childs Isbell born 2/2/1777, died 1/12/1863, married 1794

(5) great-grandson of Henry Barlow born 1726, died 1814, and his wife Judith - born 1720, died 1815, married

(6) great-grandson of Sir Thomas Barlow born / in England and came to Caroline Co. Virginia in 1695, died and

(7) great-grandson of born died and his wife born died married

(8) great-grandson of born died and his wife born died married

and he, the said Thomas Barlow II (No. 4) is the ancestor who assisted in establishing American Independence, while acting in the capacity of Private in Virginia Continental Line. Served under Lafayette and was present at the surrender at York Town.

ANCESTOR'S SERVICE

My ancestor's services in assisting in the establishment of American Independence during the War of the Revolution were as follows:

Thomas Barlow II, born in Virginia, August 25, 1760, volunteered as a Private in the Virginia Continental Line while still under age. He fought at the battle of Yorktown and was present at the surrender of Cornwallis. After the War he moved to Kentucky where he died on January 30, 1825.

National Society Sons of the American Revolution for Thomas Barlow II.

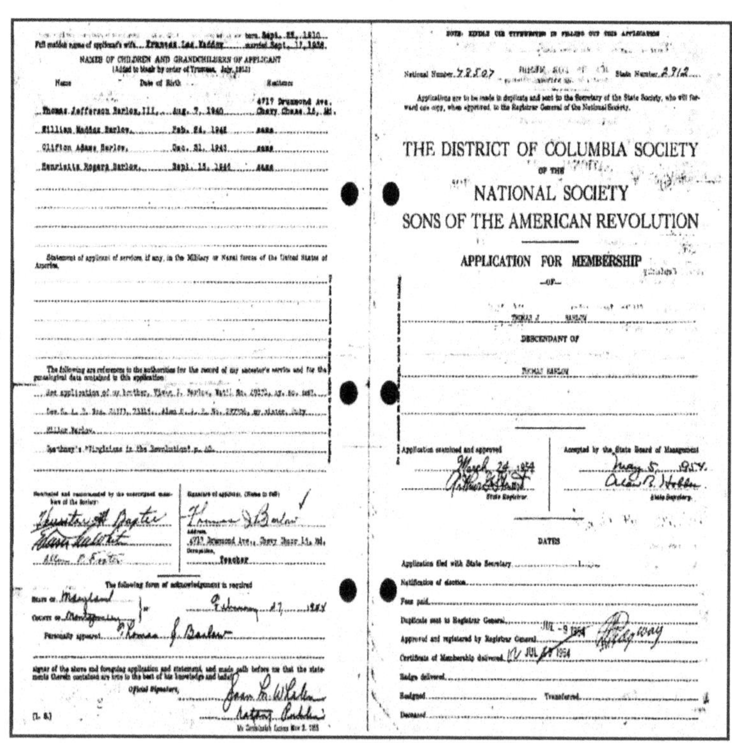

National Socity Sons of the American Revolution for Thomas J Barlow

MARRIAGE LICENSE

Virginia, *Caroline County* .... **to wit:**

To any Person Licensed to Celebrate Marriages:

You are hereby authorized to join together in the Holy State of Matrimony, according to the rites and ceremonies of your Church, or religious denomination, and the laws of the Commonwealth of Virginia, *John W. Barlow* and *Henrietta Morris*

GIVEN under my hand, as Clerk of the *County* Court of *Caroline* this *15th* day *Feby* 18*78*

Thomas W. Valentine Dy Clerk.

CERTIFICATE TO OBTAIN A MARRIAGE LICENSE.

To be Annexed to the License, required by Acts passed 15th March, 1861, and February 27th, 1866.

Time of Marriage, *About the 15th Inst*

Place of Marriage, *Caroline Co V°*

Full Names of Parties Married, *As above*

Color, *White*

Age of Husband, *34 Years*

Age of Wife, *22 "*

Condition of Husband, (widowed or single) *Single*

Condition of Wife, (widowed or single) *Single*

Place of Husband's Birth, *Caroline Co V°*

Place of Wife's Birth, *" " "*

Place of Husband's Residence, *" " "*

Place of Wife's Residence, *" " "*

Names of Husband's Parents, *Wm & Joanna Barlow*

Names of Wife's Parents, *Thos & Elizth C. N. Barlow*

Occupation of Husband, *Farmer*

Given under my hand this *15th* day of *Feby* 18*78*

Thomas W. Valentine Dy Clerk.

∽ MINISTER'S RETURN OF MARRIAGE. ∾

I Certify, That on the *13th* day of *February* 18*78* at *W. J. Self's residence* I united in Marriage the above-named and described parties, under authority of the annexed License.

John G. Rowe

☞ The Minister celebrating a marriage, is required, within ~~ten days~~ thereafter, to return the license to the Office of the Clerk who issued the same, with an endorsement thereon of the FACT of such marriage, and of the TIME and PLACE of celebrating the same.

Marriage of License for John W Barlow and Merritta Morris.

Virginia, Death Record
1912-2014

CERTIFICATE OF DEATH
COMMONWEALTH OF VIRGINIA
DEPARTMENT OF HEALTH
BUREAU OF VITAL STATISTICS

1 PLACE OF DEATH

COUNTY OF Caroline

MAGISTERIAL DISTRICT OF Bowling Green

OR INC. TOWN OF _______

OR CITY OF _______

REGISTRATION DISTRICT No. 160 B REGISTERED No. ____
(TO BE INSERTED BY REGISTRAR) (FOR USE OF LOCAL REGISTRAR)

(No. _______ St. _______ WARD)
(If death occurred in a hospital or other institution, give its NAME instead of street and number)

Length of residence in city or town where death occurred ___ yrs. ___ mos. ___ ds. How long in U. S., if foreign ___ ds.

2 FULL NAME Edmonia L. Beazley

(A) RESIDENCE. No. _______ St. _______ WARD
(Usual place of abode) (If nonresident give city or town and State)

PERSONAL AND STATISTICAL PARTICULARS

3. SEX Female

4. COLOR OR RACE White

5. SINGLE, MARRIED, WIDOWED, OR DIVORCED (write the word) Married

5A. IF MARRIED, WIDOWED, OR DIVORCED HUSBAND OF (OR) WIFE OF Thomas W. Beazley

6. DATE OF BIRTH (month, day, and year) Apr. 19, 1851

7. AGE Years 87 Months 11 Days 6 IF LESS THAN 1 DAY, ___ HRS. OR ___ MIN.

8. TRADE, PROFESSION, OR PARTICULAR KIND OF WORK DONE, AS SPINNER, SAWYER, BOOKKEEPER, ETC. Housewife

9. INDUSTRY OR BUSINESS IN WHICH WORK WAS DONE, AS SILK MILL, SAW MILL, BANK, ETC. _______

10. DATE DECEASED LAST WORKED AT THIS OCCUPATION (month and year) _______

11. TOTAL TIME (YEARS) SPENT IN THIS OCCUPATION _______

12. BIRTHPLACE (city or town) (State or country) Caroline Co., Va.

FATHER

13. NAME William Barlow

14. BIRTHPLACE (city or town) (State or country) Caroline Co., Va.

MOTHER

15. MAIDEN NAME Joan Seal

16. BIRTHPLACE (city or town) (State or country) Caroline Co., Va.

17. INFORMANT Mrs. C. E. Brooks (ADDRESS) DeJarnette, Va.

18. BURIAL, CREMATION, OR REMOVAL PLACE Providence Ch. DATE 3-26- 1939

19. UNDERTAKER Davis & Pegg (ADDRESS) Bowling Green, Va.

20. FILED _______ Registrar.

MEDICAL CERTIFICATE OF DEATH

21. DATE OF DEATH (month, day, and year) Mch 25, 1939

22. I HEREBY CERTIFY, That I attended deceased from Feb 24, 1939 to Mch 24, 1939

I LAST SAW H__ ALIVE ON Mch 24, 1939 DEATH IS SAID TO HAVE OCCURRED ON THE DATE STATED ABOVE, AT _______ M.

THE PRINCIPAL CAUSE OF DEATH AND RELATED CAUSES OF IMPORTANCE IN ORDER OF ONSET WERE AS FOLLOWS:
Senility

Date of onset

CONTRIBUTORY CAUSES OF IMPORTANCE NOT RELATED TO PRINCIPAL CAUSE:

NAME OF OPERATION _______ DATE OF _______

WHAT TEST CONFIRMED DIAGNOSIS? _______ WAS THERE AN AUTOPSY? No

23. IF DEATH WAS DUE TO EXTERNAL CAUSES (VIOLENCE) FILL IN THE FOLLOWING:
ACCIDENT, SUICIDE, OR HOMICIDE? _______ DATE OF INJURY _______

WHERE DID INJURY OCCUR? _______
(Specify city or town, county, and State)

SPECIFY WHETHER INJURY OCCURRED IN INDUSTRY, IN HOME, OR IN PUBLIC PLACE. _______

MANNER OF INJURY _______

NATURE OF INJURY _______

24. WAS DISEASE OR INJURY IN ANY WAY RELATED TO OCCUPATION OF DECEASED? No

IF SO, SPECIFY _______

(SIGNED) _______ M. D.

(ADDRESS) Bowling Green, Va.

Certificate of Death for Edmonia L Beazley.

CERTIFICATE OF DEATH
COMMONWEALTH OF VIRGINIA
DEPARTMENT OF HEALTH, BUREAU OF VITAL STATISTICS

State File No. 24454
Registered No.

Registration District No.

1. PLACE OF DEATH
a. COUNTY
MAGISTERIAL DISTRICT
b. CITY OR TOWN: Richmond — Inside Corporate Limits
c. HOSPITAL OR INSTITUTION: Medical College of Virginia
d. LENGTH OF STAY: 24 days

2. USUAL RESIDENCE (Where deceased lived. If institution: residence before admission)
a. STATE: Virginia
b. COUNTY
c. CITY OR TOWN: Richmond — Inside Corporate Limits
d. STREET ADDRESS (If rural, give mailing address): 1916 East Main St.

3. NAME OF DECEASED (Type or Print)
a. (First): Andrew
b. (Middle): Penn
c. (Last): Barlow

4. DATE OF DEATH (Month) (Day) (Year): November 10, 1949

5. SEX: Male
6. COLOR OR RACE: White
7. MARRIED, NEVER MARRIED, WIDOWED, DIVORCED (Specify): Married
8. DATE OF BIRTH: 11-23-81
9. AGE (In years last birthday): 68 [Months / Days / Hours / Min.]

10a. USUAL OCCUPATION (Give kind of work done during most of working life, even if retired): PIPE FITTER
10b. KIND OF BUSINESS OR INDUSTRY
11. BIRTHPLACE (State or foreign country): Virginia
12. CITIZEN OF WHAT COUNTRY?

13. FATHER'S NAME: Robert P. Barlow
14. MOTHER'S MAIDEN NAME: Betty L. Penn

15. NAME OF HUSBAND OR WIFE OF DECEASED: IDA
17. INFORMANT'S SIGNATURE: Medical Record, Medical College of Virginia

MEDICAL CERTIFICATION

18. CAUSE OF DEATH
Enter only one cause per line for (a), (b), and (c).
I. DISEASE OR CONDITION DIRECTLY LEADING TO DEATH
(a) Carcinoma of esophagus

ANTECEDENT CAUSES
Morbid conditions, if any, giving rise to the above cause (a) stating the underlying cause last.
DUE TO (b)
DUE TO (c)   150

II. OTHER SIGNIFICANT CONDITIONS
Conditions contributing to the death but not related to the disease or condition causing death.

INTERVAL BETWEEN ONSET AND DEATH: Unknown

19a. DATE OF OPERATION
19b. MAJOR FINDINGS OF OPERATION
20. AUTOPSY? YES ☑ NO ☐

21a. ACCIDENT, SUICIDE, HOMICIDE (Specify)
21b. PLACE OF INJURY (e.g., in or about home, farm, factory, street, office bldg., etc.)
21c. (CITY, TOWN, OR COUNTY)
(STATE)

21d. TIME OF INJURY (Month) (Day) (Year) (Hour) m.
21e. INJURY OCCURRED While at Work ☐ Not While at Work ☐
21f. HOW DID INJURY OCCUR?

22. I hereby certify that I attended the deceased from 11-1- 1949 to 11-10- 1949, that I last saw the deceased alive on 11-10-1949, and that death occurred at 4:45 p.m., from the causes and on the date stated above.

23a. SIGNATURE: Richard H. Kirkland, M.D.
(Degree or title)
23b. ADDRESS: Med. Col. of Va., Richmond, Va.
23c. DATE SIGNED: 11-10-49

24a. BURIAL, CREMATION, REMOVAL (Specify): BURIAL
24b. DATE: NOV. 12, 1949
24c. NAME OF CEMETERY OR CREMATORY: GETHSEMANE CHRISTIAN CHURCH
24d. LOCATION (City, town, or county): HANOVER CO., VIRGINIA

DATE REC'D BY LOCAL REG.: Nov. 11-1949
REGISTRAR'S SIGNATURE: O. L. Gravette

25. FUNERAL DIRECTOR'S SIGNATURE: Jos. W. Bliley Co.
ADDRESS: Richmond, Va.

Form V. S. 12

Certificate of Death for Andrew Dunn Barlow.

CERTIFICATE OF DEATH
COMMONWEALTH OF VIRGINA
Department of Health
Bureau of Vital Statistics

1. PLACE OF DEATH
County of _Henrico_ 1931
Magisterial District of _Fairfield_
Inc. Town of ____
City of ____
(No. _1625 Mosby_ St.) (If death occurred in a hospital or other institution, give its NAME instead of street and number)

Registration District No. ____ Registered No. ____
(To be inserted by Registrar) (For use of Local Registrar)

Length of residence in city or town where death occurred ____ mos. ____ ds. How long in U. S., if of foreign birth? ____ yrs. ____ mos. ____ ds.

2. FULL NAME _Charles Hagan Barlow_

(A) RESIDENCE. No. _1625 Mosby_ St. ____ Ward ____
(Usual place of abode) (If nonresident give city or town and State)

PERSONAL AND STATISTICAL PARTICULARS

3. SEX _Male_
4. COLOR OR RACE _White_
5. SINGLE, MARRIED, WIDOWED, OR DIVORCED (write the word) _Married_

5a. If married, widowed, or divorced HUSBAND of (or) WIFE of _Annie Clarke_

6. DATE OF BIRTH (month, day, and year) _Nov 23rd 1868_

7. AGE — Years _62_ | Months _1_ | Days _17_ | IF LESS THAN 1 DAY ____ HRS. OR ____ MIN.

8. TRADE, PROFESSION, OR PARTICULAR KIND OF WORK DONE, AS SPINNER, SAWYER, BOOKKEEPER, ETC. _Loco Engineer_

9. INDUSTRY OR BUSINESS IN WHICH WORK WAS DONE, AS SILK MILL, SAW MILL, BANK, ETC. _C & O. Ry Co._

10. DATE DECEASED LAST WORKED AT THIS OCCUPATION (month and year) ____
11. TOTAL TIME (YEARS) SPENT IN THIS OCCUPATION ____

12. BIRTHPLACE (city or town) _Caroline Co Va_ (State or country)

13. NAME _Robt A. Barlow_
14. BIRTHPLACE (city or town) _Caroline Co Va_ (State or country)

15. MAIDEN NAME _Bettie L Dunn_
16. BIRTHPLACE (city or town) _Caroline Co Va_ (State or country)

17. INFORMANT _Mrs C H Barlow_ (ADDRESS) _1625 Mosby St_

18. BURIAL, CREMATION, OR REMOVAL
Place _Hanover_ Date _1/10_

MEDICAL CERTIFICATE OF DEATH

21. DATE OF DEATH (month, day, and year) _January 5_ _1931_

22. I HEREBY CERTIFY, That I attended deceased from _June 10 1930_ to _Jan 8, 1931_
I last saw him alive on _Jan 5, 1931_, death is said to have occurred on the date stated above, at _10:15_

THE PRINCIPAL CAUSE OF DEATH AND RELATED CAUSES OF IMPORTANCE IN ORDER OF ONSET WERE AS FOLLOWS:

Carcinoma of Esophagus — Date of onset _?_

CONTRIBUTORY CAUSES OF IMPORTANCE NOT RELATED TO PRINCIPAL CAUSE:

NAME OF OPERATION _None_ DATE OF ____
WHAT TEST CONFIRMED DIAGNOSIS? ____ WAS THERE AN AUTOPSY? ____

23. IF DEATH WAS DUE TO EXTERNAL CAUSES (VIOLENCE) FILL IN ALSO THE FOLLOWING:
ACCIDENT, SUICIDE, OR HOMICIDE? ____ DATE OF INJURY ____
WHERE DID INJURY OCCUR? ____ (Specify city or town, county, and state)
SPECIFY WHETHER INJURY OCCURRED IN INDUSTRY, IN HOME, OR IN PUBLIC PLACE. ____
MANNER OF INJURY ____
NATURE OF INJURY ____
24. WAS DISEASE OR INJURY IN ANY WAY RELATED TO OCCUPATION OF ____

Certificate of Death for Charles Hagan Barlow.

COMMONWEALTH OF VIRGINIA — CERTIFICATE OF DEATH

DEPARTMENT OF HEALTH — BUREAU OF VITAL RECORDS AND HEALTH STATISTICS — RICHMOND

COPY A FOR BUREAU OF VITAL STATISTICS

REGISTRATION AREA NUMBER: 168
CERTIFICATE NUMBER: 12
MEDICAL EXAMINER'S CERTIFICATE
STATE FILE NUMBER: 78 003696

1. FULL NAME OF DECEASED: (first) Alice (middle) Wilbur Barlow (last) Shipp
2. SEX: female

3. DATE OF DEATH (mo.) (day) (year): Jan. 27, 1978
4. AGE OF DECEASED: 87 years
5. COLOR OR RACE: White

PLACE OF DEATH

6. NAME OF HOSPITAL OR INSTITUTION OF DEATH (if none, so state): O'FFILS Home
7. COUNTY OF DEATH (if independent city, leave blank): Orange
8. CITY OR TOWN OF DEATH (if rural, so state): Somerset — inside city or town limits? no [X]
9. STREET ADDRESS OR RT. NO. OF PLACE OF DEATH: R.F.D.

USUAL RESIDENCE OF DECEDENT

10. STATE (OR FOREIGN COUNTRY) OF DECEASED'S RESIDENCE: Virginia
11. COUNTY OF DECEASED'S RESIDENCE (if independent city, leave blank): Orange
12. CITY OR TOWN OF RESIDENCE: Barboursville — inside city or town limits? no [X]
13. STREET ADDRESS OR RT. NO. OF RESIDENCE: R.F.D. — ZIP CODE 22923

PERSONAL DATA OF DECEDENT

14. NAME OF FATHER OF DECEASED: Robert D. Barlow
15. MAIDEN NAME OF MOTHER OF DECEASED: Betty Dunn
16. DECEASED CITIZEN OF WHAT COUNTRY: U.S.A.
17. MARRIED / NEVER MARRIED / WIDOWED [X] / DIVORCED
18. IF MARRIED OR WIDOWED, NAME OF SPOUSE. IF DIVORCED, LEAVE BLANK: Leonard G. Shipp
20. IF VETERAN, name war, or if peacetime service, so state: NONE
21. BIRTHPLACE (state or country) OF DECEASED: Caroline Co., Va.
22. DATE OF BIRTH (mo.) (day) (year) OF DECEASED: April 28, 1890
23. USUAL OR LAST OCCUPATION: Housekeeping
24. KIND OF BUSINESS OR INDUSTRY: Hospital
25. INFORMANT · OR SOURCE OF INFORMATION: Miss Vergie Shipp

TO MEDICAL EXAMINER:

26. CAUSE OF DEATH (Enter only one cause per line for (A), (B), and (C).)
PART I. DEATH WAS CAUSED BY:
IMMEDIATE CAUSE (A): Coronary occlusion ?° arter.
DUE TO (B): sclerotic Heart disease — INTERVAL BETWEEN ONSET AND DEATH: <Several
DUE TO (C):

PART II. OTHER SIGNIFICANT CONDITIONS CONTRIBUTING TO DEATH BUT NOT RELATED TO THE TERMINAL DISEASE CONDITION GIVEN IN PART I (A): History recent Surgery Fracture hip ? Pulmonary embolus

26a. AUTOPSY? AUTHORIZED: no
26b. IF FEMALE, WAS THERE A PREGNANCY IN PAST 3 MONTHS? no
26c. EXTERNAL CAUSE OF DEATH WAS: PRIMARY / or CONTRIBUTING
26d. DESCRIBE HOW INJURY OCCURRED. (enter nature of injury in part I or part II)
26e. TIME OF INJURY (mo.) (day) (year) A.M. P.M.
26f. INJURY OCCURRED: while at work / not while at work
26g. PLACE OF INJURY (home, farm, factory, street, office bldg., etc.)
26h. (city or town) (county) (state)

26i. I CERTIFY that I took charge of the remains described above, viewed the body, made inquiry and in my opinion death resulted at or about 2:16 (AM) (PM) from: NATURAL CAUSES [X] / ACCIDENT / SUICIDE / HOMICIDE / UNDETERMINED / PENDING
ACTUAL SIGNATURE: W S Gobel M.D.
MEDICAL EXAMINER FOR: Orange Co. Va. (city or county)
(date signed): 2-1-78

FUNERAL DIRECTOR

27. BURIAL [X] / REMOVAL / CREMATION
28. PLACE OF BURIAL, REMOVAL, ETC.: Shipp Family Cem., Barboursville, Va.
29. (signature of funeral director or person acting as such): William J. Slaughter
NAME OF FUNERAL HOME AND ADDRESS: Preddy's Funeral Home, Gordonsville, Va.

REGISTRAR

30. (signature of registrar): Bonnie Faye Palmer
DATE RECORD FILED: 2-2-78

Certificate of Death for Alice Wilber Barlow Shipp.

H. D. V. S., Form No. 12, 200M.—6-15-12.

CERTIFICATE OF DEATH

COMMONWEALTH OF VIRGINIA
STATE BOARD OF HEALTH
Bureau of Vital Statistics

1. PLACE OF DEATH.

County of _Caroline_

District of _Bowling Green_
or
Inc. Town of __________
or
City of __________ (No. __________ St.; __________ Ward)

Registration District No. _2_

Primary Registration District No. _160_

File No. _1_

Registered No. _1_

[If death occured in a Hospital or Institution give its NAME instead of street and number.]

2. FULL NAME _John Wharton_

Residence In City ____ Yrs. ____ Mos. ____ Days ____

PERSONAL AND STATISTICAL PARTICULARS	MEDICAL CERTIFICATE OF DEATH

3. SEX _Male_ 4. COLOR OR RACE _White_ 5. SINGLE MARRIED, WIDOWED, OR DIVORCED. (Write the word) _married_

6. DATE OF BIRTH _June 14, 1832_ (Month) (Day) (Year)

7. AGE _80_ yrs. ____ mos. ____ ds. If LESS than 1 day, ____ hrs. or ____ min.?

8. OCCUPATION
(a) Trade, profession, or particular kind of work _farmer_
(b) General nature of industry, business, or establishment in which employed (or employer) __________

9. BIRTHPLACE (State or Country) _Caroline Co. Va_

PARENTS

10. NAME OF FATHER _Albert Wharton_

11. BIRTHPLACE OF FATHER (State or Country) _State of Virginia_

12. MAIDEN NAME OF MOTHER _Betsy Barlow_

13. BIRTHPLACE OF MOTHER (State or Country.) _State of Virginia_

14. THE ABOVE IS TRUE TO THE BEST OF MY KNOWLEDGE

(Informant) _Mrs Rosa Barlow_

(Address) _Shumansville Va_

15. Filed _June 27_ 1912 _Thos. W. Green_ LOCAL REGISTRAR

16. DATE OF DEATH _June 14, 1912_ (Month) (Day) (Year)

17. I HEREBY CERTIFY, That I attended deceased from _May_, 1912, to _May 8_ 1912 that I last saw him alive on _May 8_ 1912 and that death occurred, on the date stated above, at _2_ A. m. The CAUSE OF DEATH * was as follows:

Cancer of the liver

(Duration) ____ yrs. ____ mos. ____ ds.

Contributory (SECONDARY) _Catarrh of Stomach_

(Duration) ____ yrs. ____ mos. ____ ds.

(Signed) _L J Head_ M. D.

June 27, 1912 (Address) _Jerrell Va._

*State the DISEASE CAUSING DEATH, or, in deaths from VIOLENT CAUSES, state (1) MEANS OF INJURY; and (2) whether ACCIDENTAL, SUICIDAL or HOMICIDAL.

18. LENGTH OF RESIDENCE (For Hospitals, Institutions, Transients, or recent Residents
At place of death ____ yrs. ____ mos. ____ ds. In the State ____ yrs. ____ mos. ____ ds.
Where was disease contracted, if not at place of death? __________
Former or usual Residence __________

19. PLACE OF BURIAL OR REMOVAL. _Caroline Co_   DATE OF BURIAL _June 15_ 1912

20. UNDERTAKER _F. H. Pitts_   ADDRESS _Shumansville Va_

Certificate of Death for John Wharton.

THE PITTS FAMILY CORRECTIONS
& ADDITIONAL INFORMATION

Page 31 Correction	Muscoe Willis Pitts should read "Muscoe Willis Pitts Sr"
Page 31 Correction	Sally Hutchinson should read "Sarah (Sally) Hutcherson"

Page 31   Muscoe Willis Pitts Sr, b. 1783 in Caroline Co, VA, d. ___________:
m. 31 Aug 1802 to Sarah (Sally) Hutcherson, b. 1785, d. ___________.
Their issue:

1. Samuel S Pitts
2. Muscoe Willis Pitts Jr
3. Lindsey Coleman Pitts
4. Norborne Pitts should read "William Norborne (Norburn) Pitts" (See Page 132)
5. Evelina Pitts

Samuel S Pitts, b. 8 Feb 1804 in Caroline Co, VA, d. 14 Aug 1879 in OH; m. 5 Feb 1827 to Caroline Sorrel, b. c. 1806, d. ___________. They are buried in Salt Creek Cemetery, Musringum Co, OH. Their issue:

1. Warren J Pitts, b. 1833
2. George W Pitts, b. 1836
3. Sarah E Pitts, b. 1839
4. Samuel H Pitts, b. 1841
5. Martha Ann Pitts, b. 1843; m. ____________ Kelso
6. Margaret Pitts, b, 1846; m. ____________ Richardson
7. Barbary Ellen Pitts, b. 1849; m. ____________ Perrin

Page 31 Correction	Willis Pitts should read "Muscoe Willis Pitts Jr"; d. c. 1870 in Caroline Co, VA.

Page 31 Correction	Muscoe Willis Pitts Jr, b. 1806, d. c. 1870 in Caroline Co, VA; m. 28 Jan 1834 in Caroline Co, VA, to Susan Betsy Wright, b. c. 1810 in Caroline Co, VA, d. 1887 in Bowling Green, VA. Their issue:

1. Sarah Ann Pitts, b. c. 1835
2. Elizabeth (Eliza) Pitts, b. 1837
3. Martha J Pitts, b. 1841
4. George William Pitts, b. 1842
5. Robert Woodford Pitts, b. 1845
6. Mary Susan Pitts, b. 1847
7. Lucy Jane Pitts, b. 1848
8. Evelyn Pitts, b. 1851
9. Bettie G Pitts, b. 1854

NOTE: All of the children were born in Caroline Co, Shumansville, VA.

Page 35	Martha Crowe Pitts, d. 23 Feb 2009; buried in Mt Hermon Baptist Church Cemetery, Shumansville, VA

Page 37   Lillian Clayton Crowe Mitchell, m. ____________ Anthony.

Lillian Crowe Mitchell Anthony, d. 28 Jan 2012; buried in Signal Hill Memorial Park, Hanover, VA. Issue by first marriage:

1.   William Eugene Mitchell
2.   Mildred Mitchell
3.   Robert Edward Mitchell
4.   Brenda Joann Mitchell
5.   Bobby Wayne Mitchell

Page 37   George (Bucky) Swain, b. 1925, d. 8 Jun 2010; buried at sea. Bucky was the husband of Alice Crowe Swain.

Page 37   Ruby Elizabeth Crowe Kelley, d. 6 Jul 2012; buried in Signal Hill Memorial Park, Hanover, VA

Page 37   Bruce Ware Crowe, d. 9 Aug 2013. Sally Lewis Crowe, d. 27 Mar 2016. They are buried in Signal Hill Memorial Park, Hanover, VA. Their issue:

1.   Linda Crowe Witherow
2.   Kenny Crowe

They had the following grandchildren: Austin, Jordan, Jeffrey, Brittany and Nick.

Page 39   Taylor Blanton Doggett, m. 27 Oct 2018 to Caitlin Ann McClelland, b. 2 Nov 1991

Page 40   Paul Alan Cox, d. 17 Nov 2014; buried in Mt Vernon Methodist Church Cemetery, Lorne, VA

Page 42   James Jeremy Taylor, m. 27 Oct 2012 to Courtney Liane Covington, b. 7 Jun 1986. Their issue:

Sophia Mae Taylor, b. 14 Jul 2019

Page 42   Kristina Nicole Taylor, m. 4 May 2013 to Gregory Wayne Brooking, b. 2 Jul 1984. Their issue:

Tristan James Brooking, b. 16 Sep 2015

Page 42   Kasie Blair Taylor, m. 23 Jun 2018 to Zachary David Jordan, b. 18 Feb 1991

Page 43   Roger Lee Taylor, d. 24 Apr 2009; buried in Signal Hill Memorial Park, Hanover, VA

Page 44   Wilbert Lloyd Whittaker Jr, m. (2) 20 May 2009 to Mary Lee Young Pitts, b. 29 Feb 1952

Page 44   Wilma Delores Whittaker, m. (1) 1 Aug 1975 to Winston Ernest Haynes,
Correction   d. "26 Jul 1984". Winston is buried in County Line Baptist Church Cemetery, Ruther Glen, VA.

| Page 44 | David Leonard Smith, d. 4 Mar 2002; buried in County Line Baptist Church Cemetery, Ruther Glen, VA |

| Page 44 | Issue of Wilma Whittaker Smith and David Leonard Smith: |

Kendra Faith Smith

| Page 44 | Issue of Dennis Wayne Whittaker and Amy Barlow Whittaker: |

Seth Ryan Whittaker, b. 12 Sep 1994 (Adopted 26 Aug 2008)

| Page 45 | Raymond Wilson Southworth, d. 14 May 2010; buried in Wright's Burying Ground, Ruther Glen, VA |

| Page 45 Correction | George W Pitts should read "George William Pitts Sr" |

| Page 46 Correction | Lillian (Ninn) Pitts should read "Dora Lillian (Ninn) Pitts". (See page 67) |

| Page 46 Correction | Sykes Frances Trainum should read Sykes Frances "Trainham" |

| Page 46 Correction | Joseph Lennon Pitts Sr, b. 2 May 1898 at Penola, VA, d. "17 Feb 1991" in Richmond, VA; m. (1) "1920" to Addie May Lewis; m. (2) "9 Mar 1946" to Elizabeth Pleasants, b. ___________, d. "31 Oct 1995". Issue of first marriage: |

L F Pitts

Page 46   Joseph Lennon Pitts Jr, b. c. 1922, d. 28 Feb 1942

Correction   *KIA (Killed in Action)

Page 46   Betty Jo Pitts, b. ____________, m. (1) Aug 1969 to Lazaro Bolivar; m.
                    (2) 13 Apr 1990 to Lamar Sheridan. Issue by first marriage:

                    Adam Marcus Bolivar, b. 12 Mar 1970

Page 47   Virginia Lewis Beazley, d. 31 Jan 2017; buried in Lakewood Cemetery,
                    Bowling Green, VA. She had three great-grandchildren: Mavis Jordan
                    Blackley, Matthew Blackley and Margaret Rice.

Page 47   Ella Lewis Frazier, d. 4 Jan 2015

Page 47   Virginia Frazier, married ___________ Bondoc; d. ____________.

Page 47   Richard Frazier, d. ___________

Page 47   Marilyn Lewis Dyson, d. 13 Apr 2017

Page 48   Jean Marie Broaddus Rice, b. 23 Sep 1947, d. 26 Nov 1985. She is
                    buried in Signal Hill Memorial Park, Hanover, VA.

| Page 48 | Issue of Edward William Lewis and Samantha Wilcox Lewis: |

1. Harper Adalyn Lewis, b. 24 Jan 2009
2. Sutton Rose Lewis, b. 19 Jul 2011

| Page 48 | Hilary Anne Lewis, m. 1 Oct 2011 to Andrew Eugene Farnam, b. 19 Jun 1981. Their issue: |

1. Weston Robert Farnam, b. 10 Dec 2013
2. Owen Lewis Farnam, b. 1 Sep 2016

| Page 49 | Issue of Kristen Taylor Luchinsky and William Luchinsky: |

1. Garrett Lane Luchinsky, b. 16 Mar 2005
2. Strother Grayson Luchinsky, b. 7 Jun 2012

| Page 49 | Taylor Blanton Doggett, m. 27 Oct 2018 to Caitlin Ann McClelland, b. 2 Nov 1991 |

| Page 49 Correction | Isabelle Allen Monterio should read "Monteiro"; she died Dec 2007 |

| Page 49 | George Franklin Pitts' death date should read "7 Oct 1974" |

| Page 49 Correction | Mary Lavina Smith Pitts, b. "15 Nov 1912", d. "5" Apr 1994 |

Page 50   Evelyn Lavina Pitts Payne, d. 8 Jul 2004 of cancer; buried in Arlington
                        National Cemetery

Page 50   Leonard Scott was adopted by Edward Payne, second husband
Correction   of Evelyn Pitts Payne: Leonard Scott Payne

Page 50   Leonard Scott Payne, m. (1) 1976 to Dagmar Palutschik; m. (2) 1994
                        to Liz Demsey. No issue.

Page 50   Mary Raye Payne, m. 1991 to Brian Sweeney, b. 1959. Mary died
                        1 Jan 2003. Their issue:

                        Kayla Ashby Sweeney, b. 1995

Page 50   Melanie Cae Pitts, m. 1993 to Jonathan Ben Green, b. 1963.
                        Their issue:

                        1.   Dashiell Frazier Green, b. 1999
                        2.   Esme' Ramona Mollie Green, b. 2002

Page 50   David Smith Pitts, d. 10 Feb 2013; buried in Arlington National
                        Cemetery

Page 50   David Lee Pitts, m. ____________ Kolla. Their issue:

                        1.   Linda Pitts, b. 1986
                        2.   Daniel U Pitts, b. 1992

| Page 50
Correction | David Pitts should read "Mark Pitts", son of Robert Wilson Pitts. Mark married Karen ___________; they had a daughter. |

| Page 51 | Evelyn Louise Mundie Cooper, d. 18 Aug 2010 |

| Page 51 | Mallory Scott Satterwhite, m. 13 Apr 2013 to Matthew David Ganoe, b. 18 Apr 1989 |

| Page 54 | Audrey Gertrude Pitts Smith, d. Jul 2010 |

| Page 55 | George Wilbur Pitts, d. 9 Feb 2018; buried in Greenlawn Cemetery, Bowling Green, VA |

| Page 57 | Marvin Warren Pitts Jr, b. 9 Dec 1952, d. 13 Nov 2014; buried in Mt Hermon Baptist Church Cemetery, Shumansville, VA |

| Page 57
Correction | Caroline Faye Pitts should read "Carolyn". Carolyn died 28 Aug 2013. |

| Page 58
Correction | Clyde L Pitts should read Clyde "Long" Pitts "Sr". |

| Page 58 | Clyde Long Pitts Sr, m. Nancy "Maxfield". Nancy died 3 Sep 2007. |

Page 58   Nancy Pitts Vance, d. ___________

Page 58   Clyde L Pitts Jr should read Clyde "Long" Pitts Jr

Page 58   Clyde Long Pitts Jr, d. 23 Mar 2018; he is buried in Forest Lawn Cemetery, Richmond, VA. He married Diane ___________ and they had the following issue:

                        1.   Lisa Pitts; m. Jim Beggs
                        2.   Michelle Pitts
                        3.   Angela Pitts; m. Ron Windett
                        4.   Clyde Long Pitts III; m. Debbie ___________

Page 58   Doris Mae Pitts, b. 1939 in Caroline County, VA; m. Gordon Stanley

Page 58   George William Pitts should read "George William Pitts IV".
Correction

Page 58   George William Pitts IV, b. 15 Dec 1934 in Caroline County VA, d. 26 Jul 2007

Page 58   Clyde Junior Pitts, d. 15 Jan 2018; buried in Enon Baptist Church Cemetery, Supply, VA

Page 58   Jewell Fay Gallaham should read Jewell Fay "Gallahan"; Jewel Gallahan
                 Pitts, d. 9 May 2017

Page 58   Clarence James Pitts, b. 10 Apr 1946; m. (2) 25 Apr 2009 to Catherine
                 Barlow Myers, b. 9 Mar 1954

Page 59   Stephanie Kate Pitts, d. 30 Apr 1987. She was moved from Signal
                 Hill Memorial Park, Hanover, VA, to Concord Baptist Church Cemetery,
                 Ruther Glen, VA.

Page 59   Nita Lynn Pitts, b. 28 Sep 1951 in Caroline County, VA

Page 59   Robert Owen Ayers Jr, m. (3) 27 Oct 2007 in Caroline County, VA,
                 to Kimberly Ganoe

Page 60   Issue of Valerie Ayers Hall and Jason Christopher Hall:

                 1.   Christopher Ryan Hall, b. 1 Oct 2004 in Fredericksburg, VA
                 2.   Jaycob Austin Hall, b. 25 Oct 2007 in Fredericksburg, VA
                 3.   Caleb Owen Hall, b. 3 Nov 2013 in Fredericksburg, VA

Page 61   Harold Curtis Satterwhite should read "Herell"
Correction

Page 61   Randolph F Satterwhite, b. "6 Jan 1948", d. 10 Apr 2007; buried in
Correction   Virginia Veterans Cemetery, Amelia, VA

Page 61   Roderick O Satterwhite, d. 29 Mar 2008; buried in Winns Baptist
                         Church Cemetery, Glen Allen, VA. Issue:

                         1.   Jonathan Satterwhite
                         2.   Justin Satterwhite

Page 61   Clarence Burton Satterwhite and Clarence Broaddus Satterwhite
Correction   are one and the same person. Clarence was b. 19 Mar 1918, d. 1
                         Feb 2007. He married Dec 1942 to Rosa Ellen Buchanan, b. 1920,
                         d. 20 Feb 2012. They are buried in Taylorsville Baptist Church
                         Cemetery, Doswell VA.

Page 61   Linda Sue Satterwhite Thompson Taylor, d. 2 Oct 2011

Page 62   James Leon Allen, d. 19 May 2010; buried in Salem Baptist Church
                         Cemetery, Sparta, VA

Page 62   Frances Satterwhite Allen, d. 22 May 2017; buried in Salem Baptist
                         Church Cemetery, Sparta, VA

Page 63   Claude Anderson Satterwhite Jr, d. 11 Sep 2014; buried in Washington
                         Memorial Park, Richmond, VA

Page 63   Margaret Satterwhite Woods, d. 20 Jan 2016

Page 63   Dennis Leon Jarrell, d. ____________

Page 65   William Gordon Taylor, d. 10 Jun 2008; buried in Signal Hill Memorial
                 Park, Hanover, VA

Page 67   Lillian N Pitts should read "Dora Lillian (Ninn) Pitts".
Correction

Page 67   Dora Lillian (Ninn) Pitts, b. 7 Jun 1890 in Caroline Co, VA, d. 22 Aug
                 1962 in Baltimore, MD; m. (1) 4 Sep 1907 to Archie Thomas South-
                 worth, b. 28 Jul 1886 in Caroline County, VA, d. 4 Feb 1935 in
                 Hanover, VA; m. (2) James M England. Lillian in buried under the
                 name of Lillian L England in Baltimore, MD. Issue by first marriage:

                 1.   Bettie Lillian Southworth
                 2.   Herman Lee Southworth
                 3.   Clyde George Southworth
                 4.   Gladys Elizabeth Southworth

Page 67   Bettie Lillian Southworth, b. 9 Dec 1910 in Ashland, VA, d. 8 Jan 2006
Correction   in PA; m. (1) 16 Mar 1931 to William Lawrence Binns, b. 1907, d.
                 1987; m. (2) 8 Jan 1938 to Edmund Gwynn Coe Jr, b. 1912, d. 1966;
                 m. (3) George H Sprague, b. 1910, d. 1982. Bettie is buried in Loudon
                 Park Cemetery in PA. She was survived by four grandchildren and
                 five great grandchildren. Issue by second marriage:

                 1.   Bettie Helen Coe
                 2.   Edmund Gwynn Coe III

                 Bettie Helen Coe, b. 9 Dec 1934 in Evansville, IN, d. 2015; m.
                         ____________ Dailey

Page 67   Herman Lee Southworth, b. 1 Apr 1914 in Caroline Co, VA, d. Sep 1981 in Baltimore, MD; m. 23 Mar 1935 to Helen Earle Yarbrough, b. 1914, d. 1999. Their issue:

1.   James Barton Southworth
2.   Herman Lee Southworth Jr
3.   Deborah A Southworth

James Barton Southworth, b. 1936; m. Rose Moore

Herman Lee Southworth Jr, b. 1938

Deborah A Southworth, b. 1956; m. John Hurman

Page 67   Clyde George Southworth, b. 20 Mar 1919 in Doswell, VA, d. 21
Correction   Jul 2004

Page 67   Gladys Elizabeth Southworth, b. 21 Sep 1926 in Richmond, VA, d. 12 May 1995; m. ___________ Smith. Gladys is buried beside her mother in Baltimore, MD.

Page 68   Gertrude Pitts Thomas, d. 16 Aug 2016; buried in Newport News, VA

Page 68   Adam Thomas Carnegie, m. 29 Nov 2008 to Karen (Kacey) Robbins. Their issue:

Ellison Carol Carnegie, b. 4 Mar 2014 in Norfolk, VA

Page 68   Alice Carroll Carnegie, m. David Paul Harris. Their issue:

1. Easton Taylor Harris, b. 28 Mar 2013 in Suffolk, VA
2. Blake Lambert Harris, b. 29 Aug 2017 in Suffolk, VA

Page 68   Aaron William Carnegie, m. Sandra Collick. Their issue:

Bryce William Carnegie, b. 20 Oct 2012 in Suffolk, VA

Page 68   Carroll Lawrence (Billy) Pitts, d. 29 May 2010 in Richmond, VA; buried in Mt Hermon Baptist Church Cemetery, Shumansville, VA

Page 69   Lelia Floyd Pitts Loving, d. 19 Sep 2008 in Richmond, VA; buried in Mt Hermon Baptist Church Cemetery, Shumansville, VA

Page 69   Jeanne Pitts Tolley, d. 1 Jul 2011; buried in Westhampton Memorial Park, Richmond, VA

Page 70   Laura Elizabeth Hoke, b. 15 Dec 1979; m. 2 Apr 2005 to Michael Armstrong. Their issue:

Ian Thomas Armstrong, b. 13 Aug 2009

Page 70   Sarah Rebecca Hoke, m. Nick Colley

Page 70   Thomas Christian Tolley, b. 1 Aug 1957; m. 17 Sep 1983 to Linda
                       Louise Wilkins, b. 19 Dec 1951. Their issue:

                       1.   Megan Kathryn Tolley, b. 25 Sep 1986
                       2.   Meredith Christian Tolley, b. 17 Jul 1989

Page 70   William Maynard Carter Sr, d. 12 Aug 2011; buried in Greenlawn
                       Cemetery, Bowling Green, VA

Page 70   Cooper Grayson Townsend should read Cooper "Franklyn" Townsend
Correction

Page 71   Issue of Kenneth Stephen Stewart Jr and Susan Guess Stewart:

                       1.   Kaylie Elizabeth Stewart, b. 7 Mar 2006
                       2.   Madison Ann Stewart, b. 2 Dec 2008

Page 71   Issue of Jamie Farmer Burton and Joseph Wade Burton:

                       1.   Josie Wray Burton, b. 30 Sep 2007
                       2.   Cayden James Burton, b. 3 Jun 2010) Twins
                       3.   Carter Joseph Burton, b. 3 Jun 2010)

Page 71   Meredith Ryan Lane Carter's birthdate should read "25" Apr "1977".

Page 71   Issue of William Maynard Carter III and Meredith Ryan Lane Carter:

1. William Maynard Carter IV, b. 23 Feb 2005
2. Harrison Lane Carter, b. 3 May 2007
3. Graham Patrick Carter, b. 16 Sep 2011
4. Mary Katherine Spencer Carter, b. 1 Mar 2017

Page 71   Jennifer Meade Carter, m. (2) 13 May 2008 to Chip Hartle. Issue by second marriage:

1. Ella Grace Hartle, b. 14 May 2009
2. Kaelynn Hope Hartle, b. 26 Mar 2012

Page 71   Scott Tyler Pitts, m. Jennifer ___________. Their issue:

Kieran Ryan Pitts, b. 16 Mar 2010

Page 72   Cordie Gatewood Pitts, d. 13 Apr 2007

Page 72   Mary Gatewood Pitts, d. 27 Feb 2007

Page 72   Ann Pitts Hagerty, d. 13 Mar 2015; buried in PA

Page 72   Charles Lewis Hagerty, d. 23 May 2008, buried in PA

Page 73   Donald James Pitts, d. 25 Dec 2015; buried in Salem Baptist Church Cemetery, Sparta, VA

Page 73   Joshua Dwayne Watts, m. 28 Jun 2000 to Brandy Michelle Perry, b.
               9 Feb 1979. Their issue:

               1.   Courtney Grace Watts, b. 9 Aug 2007) Twins
               2.   Charles Tucker Watts, b. 9 Aug 2007)

Page 73   Jared Hugh Watts, m. 8 Dec 2007 to Whitney Sterling Schoonover,
               b. 28 Jan 1985. Their issue:

               1.   Kennedy Sterling Watts, b. 26 Mar 2013
               2.   Reese Aileen Watts, b. 13 Jan 2016
               3.   Walker Hugh Watts, b. 29 Aug 2018

Page 73   Burle Daniel (Danny) Trivette's birthdate should read "7" Nov "1962".
Correction

Page 73   Issue of Dawn Pitts Trivette and Burle Daniel (Danny) Trivette:

               1.   James Austin Trivette, b. 9 Oct 1991
               2.   Jason Daniel Trivette, b. 17 Jan 1994
               3.   Jacob Robert Trivette, b. 4 Dec 1995

Page 73   Dawn Pitts Trivette, m. (2) 25 May 2011 to Roy A Haun, b. 11 Dec 1971

Page 73   James Austin Trivette, d. 9 Apr 2013; buried in Salem Baptist Church
               Cemetery, Sparta, VA

Page 74	Jennifer Leigh Pitts, d. 18 Jun 2008
Page 75	Phyllis Babcock Pitts, d. 19 Sep 2010
Page 75	Charles Eugene Pitts, b. 12 Jul 1930, d. 11 Jan 2006; buried in Gloucester Point Cemetery, Gloucester, VA
Page 75	John Ashby Loving, d. 16 Apr 2011; buried in Signal Hill Memorial Park, Hanover, VA
Page 76	Wilbert Lloyd Whittaker Jr, m. (2) 20 May 2009 to Mary Lee Young Pitts, b. 29 Feb 1952
Page 76 Correction	Wilma Delores Whittaker, m. (1) 1 Aug 1975 to Winston Ernest Haynes, d. "26 Jul 1984". Winston is buried in County Line Baptist Church Cemetery, Ruther Glen, VA.
Page 76	David Leonard Smith, d. 4 Mar 2002; buried in County Line Baptist Church Cemetery, Ruther Glen
Page 76	Issue of Wilma Whittaker Smith and David Leonard Smith: Kendra Faith Smith

Page 76   Issue of Dennis Wayne Whittaker and Amy Barlow Whittaker:

Seth Ryan Whittaker, b. 12 Sep 1994 (Adopted 26 Aug 2008)

Page 77   Marcia Pitts Englert, d. 21 Mar 2018 in Richmond, VA; buried in Greenwood Memorial Gardens, Goochland, VA

Page 77   Issue of Ardis Burford Fishburne and James Gahan Fishburne Jr:

1.   Catherine Christine Fishburne, b. 12 Jul 2000 in Richmond, VA
2.   James Gahan Fishburne III, b. 18 Sep 2002 in Richmond, VA
3.   Robert Douglas Fishburne, b. 20 Jul 2007 in Richmond, VA

Page 77   John Jason Burford, m. 17 Apr 2004 to Amy Suzanne Harrell, b. 2 Aug 1976. Their issue:

1.   John Thomas Burford, b. 24 Feb 2009 in Richmond, VA
2.   Caroline Batson Burford, b. 15 Apr 2011 in Richmond, VA

Page 77   Jocelyn Hilton Pitts, m. 10 Oct 2010 to Gary John Lowzik Jr, b. 10 Feb 1979. Their issue:

Emily Alexis Lowzik, b. 4 Nov 2018 in Richmond, VA

Page 77   Mariano (Gus) Taormina, d. 22 Sep 2013

Page 77   Mary Pitts Taormina, m. (3) 7 May 2017 to Lawson John Heggie, b. 10 Feb 1954

Page 77   Tina Marie Embrey Pitts, d. 7 Feb 2017

Page 77   Alesia Ann St Clair Pitts, d. ___________

Page 78   Jeremy Scott Pitts' birthdate should read "4 Jun 1977"
Correction

Page 78   Jeremy Scott Pitts, m. (1) 29 Sep 2007 to Laura Angeline Marsh; m. (2) 3 Dec 2015 to Brandy Nicole Wade, b. 12 Oct 1976. Issue by second marriage:

                   Ashton Wade Pitts, b. 22 Feb 2014

Page 78   Bernard Randolph Pitts, d. 22 Dec 2009: buried in Salem Baptist Church Cemetery, Sparta, VA

Page 78   Arthur Herman Witmeyer, d. 13 Jun 2013; buried in Quantico National Cemetery

Page 78   Sarah Almeda Pitts, m. Ryan Colvin on 11 Aug 2007. Their issue:

                   1. Randolph Barrett (Rett) Colvin, b. 31 Jul 2011
                   2. Ryland Bruce (Riley) Colvin, b. 25 Aug 2013

3.   Caroline Elizabeth Colvin, b. 26 Aug 2016

4.   Robert Burton (Robbie) Colvin, b. 5 Apr 2018

Page 78   Issue of Anne Pitts Grove and Jacob Landon Grove:

1.   Charlotte Anne Grove, b. 16 Apr 2012

2.   Jack Randolph Grove, b. 10 Oct 2014

Page 79   Jennifer Carol Pitts, m. 22 Oct 2016 to Matthew Scott Anns, b. 16
                 Apr 1987. Her issue:

Adam James Pitts, b. 31 Jan 2006

Their issue:

Lily Grace Anns, b. 23 Apr 2018

Page 79   Christopher Nelson Pitts, m. 2 May 2015 to Laura Owens, b. 24 Oct
                 1988. Their issue:

1.   Levi Owen Pitts, b. 10 Jan 2017

2.   Caleb Nelson Pitts, b. 27 Sep 2018

Page 79   David Sterling Ganoe Jr, d. 17 Nov 2006: buried in Salem Baptist Church
                 Cemetery, Sparta, VA

Page 79   Matthew David Ganoe, m. 13 Apr 2013 to Mallory Scott Satterwhite,
                 b. 19 Sep 1988

Page 79	Melissa Jaclyn Ganoe, m. 22 Jul 2017 to Tucker Wayne Brown
Page 80	Joyce Pitts Wilson, d. 16 Apr 2018; buried in County Line Baptist Church Cemetery, Ruther Glen, VA
Page 80	Robin Elizabeth Wilson , d. 19 May 1970. She was moved from Central Baptist Church Cemetery, Richmond, VA, to County Line Baptist Church Cemetery, Ruther Glen, VA.
Page 80	Marion Joyce Kelley Baughan, d. 17 Dec 2014; buried in St. Stephen's Baptist Church Cemetery, St. Stephen's Church, VA
Page 82 Correction	Neale Wayne Kelley's birth date should read 10 May "1949". Neale Wayne Kelley, d. 25 Jun 2017; cremated
Page 82	Jacquelin Pleasants Kelley, d. 8 Nov 2014
Page 82	Stephanie Ryan Covington, m. (2) 4 Apr 2015 to Benjamin Jeffrey-Preece Sadler, b. 2 Nov 1987
Page 82	Karla Renee Covington, m. 12 May 2018 to Ryan Perry Eutsler, b. 30 Jul 1985

Page 82   Courtney Liane Covington, m. 27 Oct 2012 to James Jeremy Taylor, b. 2 Dec 1982. Their issue:

Sophia Mae Taylor, b. 14 Jul 2019

Page 83   Krista Lynn Gill should read "Krysta" Lynn Gill

Page 83   Issue of Krysta Lynn Gill and Jonathan Art Jackson:

Jocelyn Avery Jackson, b. 15 Dec 2013 in Raleigh, NC

Page 83   Issue of Meagan Renee Gill and Ashley Kyle Beamon:

Bryce Mason Beamon, b. 18 Sep 2014 in Raleigh, NC

Page 83   Andrew Michael Gill, m. 15 Oct 2005 to Christy Michelle Warren. Their issue:

1. Taylor Lee-Ann Gill, b. 6 Aug 2003
2. Peyton Sue Gill, b. 17 May 2008

Page 83   Robert Carroll Beazley III, m. 18 Oct 2008 to Valerie Basoco. Their issue:

1. Robert Carroll Beazley IV, b. 3 Jan 2009 in CA
2. Summer Valentina Beazley, b. 19 Aug 2010 in CA

Page 83   Mark Alan Beazley, m. 9 May 2009 to Amber Nicole Link. Their issue:

Delaney Lynn Beazley, b. 1 Mar 2010 in Newport News, VA

Page 84   Issue of Johanna Elizabeth Beazley:

               Bailey Elizabeth Tilley, b. 29 Jul 2009

Page 84   Lillian Pitts Pugh Pavy, d. 29 Nov 2016; buried in Mt Hermon Baptist
               Church Cemetery, Shumansville, VA

Page 84   Robert Woodford (Dick) Pitts, d. 29 May 2018; buried in Mt Hermon
               Baptist Church Cemetery, Shumansville, VA

Page 84   Issue of Taylor Madeline Roberts:

               Karson Deaton, b. 26 Dec 2013

Page 84   Issue of Christopher Lanny Fulford and Crystal Wilder Fulford:

               Chase Wyatt Fulford, b. 17 Jun 2007

Page 85   Katherine Louise Phillips, m. 20 Jun 2015 to Chad Devine, b. ___________.

               Issue of Katherine (Katie) Phillips Devine and Bryan Marzo:

               Everly Katherine Marzo, b. 8 Feb 2019

Page 85   Joseph James Hartman, d. 15 Dec 2006; buried in Holy Cross
                 Cemetery, Cleveland, OH

Page 85   Ian James McHugh, m. (1) 19 Aug 2008 to Tami H Brown; m. (2) 20
                 Jul 2018 to Betsy Woods Lenahan, b. 25 May 1979. Issue by first
                 marriage:

                 Neala Dolly McHugh, b. 8 Dec 2014 in CA

Page 85   Nellie Ann McHugh, m. 15 Jul 2017 to Tyler Wade Tingley, b. 30 Sep
                 1977. Their issue:

                 Owen Ronald Tingley, b. 17 May 2018 in OH

Page 86   Issue of John David Hartman and Michelle Hornbeck Hartman:

                 1. John Carter (Jack) Hartman, b. 31 Jul 2006 in Chicago, IL
                 2. Henry Joseph Hartman, b. 22 Oct 2009 in Chicago, IL

Page 86   Edward Dawson Pitts, d. 26 Nov 2011: cremated

Page 86   Mabel Pitts Weymouth, d. 1 Oct 2018; buried in Mt Hermon Baptist
                 Church Cemetery, Shumansville, VA

Page 86   Julian Roy (Big Boy) Carter Sr, d. 13 Dec 2018; buried in Greenlawn
                 Cemetery, Bowling Green, VA

Page 86   Lisa Kay Carter Burch, m (2) 21 Nov 2009 to John Woodroof. Issue
               by second marriage:

               Julianne Isabella Woodroof, b. 1 Feb 2011

Page 86   Benny Sale Brooks, d. 1 Sep 2016; cremated

Page 86   Jonathan Benjamin Brooks, m. 4 Jun 2016 to Lauren Elizabeth Didlake,
               b. 23 Sep 1991. Their issue:

               Carter Elizabeth Brooks, b. 9 May 2017 in Richmond, VA

Page 87   Irene Zicafoose Pitts, d. 2 Feb 2011 in Ashland, VA; buried in Mt
               Hermon Baptist Church Cemetery, Shumansville, VA

Page 87   Issue of John Eric Oakes and Kellie Gardner Oakes:

               1. Everett Liam Gardner Oakes, b. 15 Mar 2013 in ME
               2. Fianna Elsie Andalyn Oakes, b. 12 Nov 2015 in ME

Page 87   Michael Brandon Oakes, m. 31 Oct 2008 to Rachel Feero, b. 24 Mar
               1981. Their issue:

               1. Oscar Malcolm Eastwood Oakes, b. 19 Feb 2008 in ME
               2. Emerson Enzo Feero Oakes, b. 8 Apr 2010 in ME
               3. Tesla River Violet Oakes, b. 9 Apr 2015 in ME

Page 87   Katie Lea Oakes, m. 26 Jul 2008 to Conor McMahon, b. 15 Aug 1978. Their issue:

1.   Virginia June Oakes McMahon, b. 14 Oct 2009 in NM
2.   Cassius Owen Oakes McMahon, b. 29 Jan 2012 in KY

Page 87   Issue of Scott Andrew Oakes and Dora Bowden Oakes:

1.   Kolee Mae Oakes, b. 13 Nov 2002 in Waterville, ME
2.   Brandon Zane Oakes, b. 18 Nov 2006 in ME

Issue of Scott Andrew Oakes and Shannon Marie Alexander, b. 21 Sep 1989:

Landon Roger Alexander, b. 2 Jul 2009 in ME

Issue of Scott Andrew Oakes and Twanic Poliquin:

Alexiyah Poliquin, b. 24 Aug 2011 in ME

Page 87   Rebecca Lynn Oakes, m. 5 Nov 2011 to Timothy Dean DeWitt, b. 9 Jun 1981. Their issue:

1.   Hannah Lea Oakes, b. 29 Jul 2006 in ME
2.   Norah Elizabeth Oakes, b. 7 Oct 2010 in ME
3.   Carter Dean DeWitt, b. 30 Apr 2012 in ME

Page 87   Sarah Elizabeth Edwards, m. 25 May 2013 to Stephen Michael Salvato. Their issue:

Page 100   Effie Carr Pitts Crowell, d. 1 Jan 1937

Page 101   Jackson Howard Crowell should read "Jack Howell" Crowell "Sr"
Correction

Page 101   Issue of Jack Howell Crowell Sr and Effie Sale Toombs Crowell:

                  Jack Howell Crowell Jr, b. 17 Dec 1948, d. 4 Mar 2019; buried in
                  Lakewood Cemetery, Bowling Green, VA

Page 101   John H Crowell should read John "Henry" Crowell
Correction

Page 101   Issue of John Henry Crowell and Helen Brown Crowell:

                  1. John Henry Crowell Jr
                  2. Willard Ray Crowell

Page 101   Willard Morris Crowell Jr, b. 21 Jun 1918; m. 1953 to Effie Sale
                  Toombs Crowell

Page 103   Clara Lee (Lizzie) Pitts, b. "25 Jul 1884" in Caroline County, VA; d.
Correction   2 Sep 1969 in Petersburg, VA

Page 103   Andrew (Jew) Pitts, b. 14 Sep 1886; m. Estelle Pitts

Page 104   William Arthur Claytor Jr, d. 30 May 2007

| Page 104 | John Earl Claytor, b, 11 Jan 1916, d. 3 Dec 1935 at Bagby, VA |

| Page 104 Correction | Harry Francis Claytor Sr," b. 23 Jun 1919, d. 11 Jun 2003" |

| Page 105 | Lucy Pitts, b. 18 Jun 1889; follows Ruth Pitts on Page 105 |

| Page 111 | Lucille Langford Tucker, b. 10 Nov 1926, d. 6 Sep 2007; buried in Bruington Baptist Church Cemetery, King and Queen Co, VA |

| Page 111 Correction | Milton Lee Tucker Sr's birthdate should read "4 Aug 1926" |

| Page 111 | Issue of Milton Lee Tucker Jr and Anne Fogg Tucker:
Jason Tuckekr b. ___________ |

| Page 111 Correction | Issue of Milton Lee Tucker Jr & Karen Tucker:

1. Teresa Tucker, b. ___________
2. Steffan Tucker, b. ___________ |

| Page 111 | Jean Maria Carter Langford , d. 3 Apr 2012; buried in Greenlawn Cemetery, Bowling Green, VA |

| Page 111 | Issue of Robert Lee Langford and Jean Carter Langford: |

1. Cheryl Ann Langford
2. Kevin Lee Langford
3. Pamela Jean Langford

Page 112   Cheryl Ann Langford, b. 16 Jan 1960; m. 20 Feb 1976 to Charles Raymond Brooks, b. 28 Jul 1956: Their issue:

1. Teresa Jean Brooks
2. Charles Raymond (Chad) Brooks Jr

Teresa Jean Brooks, b. 11 Aug 1976; m. 29 Aug 1997 to John Robert Skinner. Their issue:

1. Devin Ray Skinner, b. 4 Feb 1997
2. Alexis Ann Skinner, b. 4 Oct 2002

Charles Raymond (Chad) Brooks Jr, b. 12 Mar 1982; m. 10 Sep 2011 to Anne Stuart Curran, b. 31 Dec 1985. Their issue:

1. Chandler Elizabeth Brooks, b. 23 Mar 2013
2. Adelynn Stuart Brooks, b. 19 Jun 2016

Page 111   Kevin Lee Langford, b. 7 Dec 1962; m. Teresa Pointer. Their issue:

Dylan Langford

Page 112   Pamela Jean Langford, b. 1 Sep 1965; m. (1) 15 Sep 1984 to Ralph Steven Trainham; m. (2) 10 May 2004 to Craig Arnold Knepp. Issue from first marriage:

Robert Trainham

Robert Trainham, b. 24 Apr 1987. Issue:

1. Nathan Trainham
2. Chesney Trainham

Page 112
Correction

James Dennis Martin (husband of Bessie Mae Langford Martin) should read "James Arthur" Martin. His birthdate should read 20 Sep "1930"; d. 2 Feb 2002; buried in Upper Essex Baptist Church Cemetery, Champlain, VA

Page 112

Bessie Langford Martin, m. (2) 5 Jul 2003 to Gilbert Eugene Gallagher, b. 25 May 1936

Page 112

Deborah Faye Martin, m. 25 Aug 1978 to Duane Scott Coghill, b. 19 Mar 1952. Their issue:

1. Jessica Scott Coghill
2. James Scott Coghill, b. 22 Sep 1987

Jessica Scott Coghill, b. 16 Apr 1979; m. 18 Aug 2007 to Vincent Craig Revels, b. 2 Jun 1971. Their issue:

1. Ella Grace Revels, b. 16 Dec 2009
2. Vincent Leyton Revels, b. 24 Mar 2011

Page 112

James Dennis Martin Jr should read "Dennis James Martin." Dennis

Correction   James Martin, b. 26 Jan 1965, d. 3 Jan 2014; m. 20 May 1994 to
                    Darlene Sydnor Mitchell, b. 13 Oct 1954. Their issue:

                    Katie Lynn Martin, b. 15 Jul 1997

Page 112   Laura Elizabeth Langford, m. (1) ___________ Smith; m. (2) Joseph
Correction   Bruce Norman. Issue from first marriage:

                    1. Jimmy Fomax Smith
                    2. Timmy Lewis Smith

                    Issue from second marriage:

                    Kimberly Norman

Page 121   Edna Irene Gray Pitts, b." 4 May 1922", d. 13 Jul 2012
Correction

Page 123   Thelma Pitts Priddy, d. 27 Nov 2010; buried in Kenwood Methodist
                    Church Cemetery

Page 123   Issue of Crystal LaVoie Lang and Wallace Cabell Lang III:

                    1. Helen Dabney Lang, b. 23 Jun 2004
                    2. Frances Madeleine Lang, b. 11 Oct 2005
                    3. ___________, b. 2007
                    4. Griffin Lavoie Lang, b. 11 May 2009

Page 124   Thomas Lee Rice, m. Virginia Woody

Page 124   Bernard "F" Pitts, b. 1936, d. 4 Mar 2007; m. Mitzie Davis. Bernard
                  is buried in Signal Hill Memorial Park, Hanover, VA. Their issue:

                  1.   Steven W Pitts
                  2.   Sheryl Pitts

Page 124   Steven W Pitts, m. Donna ___________. Their issue:

                  1.   Benjamin Pitts
                  2.   Brian Pitts

Page 124   Sheryl Pitts, m. Barry Smart. Issue by first marriage:

                  1.   Christina Zahn
                  2.   Casey Zahn

Page 125   John Wayne Pitts, b. 13 Feb 1949, d. 5 Sep 2010; m. Joyce Pitts.
                  John is buried in Killeen, TX. Their issue:

                  1.   Joyce Anne Pitts
                  2.   John Wayne Pitts Jr

Page 128   Norma Cecil Claytor, d. 9 Mar 2014; buried in Signal Hill Memorial
                  Park, Hanover, VA

Page 128   Edward Leslie Claytor, d. 24 Oct 2007; buried in Signal Hill Memorial Park, Hanover, VA

Page 128   Issue of Nathan Lee Hill and Elizabeth Vaughan Hill:

1. Breelan Grace Hill, b. 25 Apr 2005
2. Thomas Jackson Hill, b. ___________

Page 132   Norborne (Norman) Pitts should read "William Norborne (Norburn)"
Correction   Pitts.

Page 132   William Norborne (Norburn) Pitts (Farmer), b. c. 1812 in Caroline
Correction   Co, VA, d. ___________; m. 23 Oct 1839 to (1) Malinda Moran, b. c. 1821, d. ___________; m. (2) Lucy Murray, b. c. 1841, on 8 Nov 1866 in Caroline Co, VA, by Rev Andrew Broaddus Jr. Norborne, age 54, was a widower when he married Lucy, age 25. Issue by first marriage:

1. Sarah Pitts
2. Richard A Pitts
3. Oteria Ann Pitts
4. Lucinda Pitts
5. Tenah Loven Pitts
6. Mary Ella Pitts
7. William Norborne Pitts Jr

Issue by second marriage:

1. Daniel John Pitts
2. Addie Lee Pitts

3. Mary Pitts

4. Nannie Beatrice Pitts

Page 132   Sarah Pitts, b. c. 1840 in Caroline Co, VA, d. ____________; m. 4 Sep
1858 to John L ____________, b. ____________

Page 132   Richard A Pitts (Farmer), b. 19 Feb 1842 in Caroline Co, VA, d. 28
Feb 1914; m. 27 Jul 1865 in Essex Co, VA, by Rev E B McGuire to
Alice Vawter, b. 2 Oct 1848, d. 24 Mar 1915. They are buried in
Essex Co, VA.

Page 132   Oteria Ann Pitts, b. c. 1843 in Caroline Co, VA, d. 1911; m. 14 Dec
1865 by R W Cole to Bird (Byrd) Loving, b. c. 1842, d. ____________.
They were married at John Loving's home.

Page 132   Lucinda Pitts, b. May 1846 in Caroline Co, VA, d. c. 1930; m. 26 Dec
1867 to Allen Loving, b. c. 1848, d. ____________. They were
married by Rev R C Cole in Caroline Co, VA. Their issue:

1.   Scott A Loving, b. 16 Aug 1874, d. 21 Jan ____________

2.   Dolly Loving, b. Sep 1878, d. ____________

3.   Molly Loving, b. May 1880, d. ____________

4.   Nellie Gray Loving, b. 9 Jul 1883 in King & Queen Co, VA, d.
15 Sep 1950 in King & Queen Co, VA

Page 132   Tenah Loven Pitts, b. 1851 in King & Queen Co, VA, d. ____________;
m. 11 Jul 1891 to Robert W Taylor, b. 1831, d. ____________

Mary Ella Pitts, b. c. 1852, d. ___________; m. 13 May 1878 to Patrick H Harper, b. 1843, d. ___________. They were married by Rev James H Marshall.

William Norborne Pitts Jr (Farmer), b. Jul 1853 in Caroline Co, VA, d. 1 Jul 1919 in Bagby, VA, of epileptic convulsions caused by a weakened heart; m. 1 Feb 1877 to Ida Elizabeth Coghill, b. Mar 1853 in Essex Co, VA, d. 20 Mar 1928 in Petersburg, VA. They were married at the home of Richard Vawter in Essex Co, VA, by Rev Alexander Overby. William is buried near his home in Bagby, VA. Their issue:

1. John C Pitts
2. Allen (Allie) Pitts
3. Sallie Anne Pitts
4. William F Pitts
5. Betty T (Bell) Pitts
6. James Arthur Pitts
7. Lucy T Pitts
8. Louisa Pitts
9. Sooner Arville Pitts
10. Scott Hampton Pitts
11. Emogene (Imogene) Pitts

John C Pitts, b. 15 Jun 1881 in Essex, Co, VA, d. 14 Jul 1935; m. 30 Oct 1901 to Kittie A Martin, b. 1878, d. ___________. They are buried in Salem Baptist Church Cemetery, Sparta, VA.

Allen (Allie) Pitts, b. 1883 in Caroline Co, VA, d. 25 Sep 1918 in Caroline Co, VA; m. 20 Jul 1904 to Bettie Pitts, b. Apr 1883 in Caroline Co, VA, d. ___________. Their issue:

Teresa Bernice Pitts, b. 27 Jul 1912 in Caroline Co, VA, d. ___________

Page 132   Sallie Anne Pitts, b. May 1884 in Essex Co, VA, d. 28 Sep 1918 in Caroline Co, VA; m. 10 Apr 1901 to Benjamin Cecil, b. 1875, d. ___________

Page 132   William F Pitts, b. Mar 1885, d. ___________; m. 9 May 1906 in Caroline Co, VA, to Carrie Beasley, b. 1889, d. ___________

Page 132   Betty T (Bell) Pitts, b. c. 1888, d. 5 May 1940 at Point Eastern, VA

Page 132   James Arthur Pitts, b. 24 Feb 1890 in Caroline Co, VA, d. 5 Oct 1917 in Caroline Co, VA; m. 2 Dec 1909 to Mattie Louise Doggett, b. c. 1893,d. 9 Apr 1980. She is buried in Forest Lawn Cemetery, Richmond, VA.

Page 132   Lucy T Pitts, b. 13 Dec 1892 in Essex Co, VA, d. 29 Dec 1894 of infant cholera in Essex Co, VA

Page 132   Louisa Pitts, b. 20 Aug 1894 in Essex Co, VA, d. 20 Dec 1894 of brain fever in Essex Co, VA

Page 132   Sooner Arville (Alvill) Pitts, b. c. 1898, d. 19 May 1924 in Petersburg, VA; m. 19 Nov 1921 to Ruth Virginia Nunnally

Page 132   Scott Hampton Pitts, b. 25 Jul 1899, d. 25 Dec 1935 of pulmonary tuberculosis; m. 14 Feb 1917 in Bowling Green, VA, to Melinda Ella Moore, b. c. 1900, d.___________

Page 132

Emogene (Imogene) Pitts, b. 8 Jun 1905 in Essex Co, VA, d. 10 Jan 1968 in Colonial Heights, VA

Page 132

Daniel John Pitts, b. Jun 1867 in Caroline Co, VA, d. ___________; m. 9 Jan 1906 to Mary Vortis, b. ___________

Page 132

Addie Lee Pitts, b. 1873, d. ___________; m. ___________ Crouch. Had issue of one daughter.

Page 132

Mary Pitts, b. 1877, d. ___________

Page 132

Nannie Beatrice Pitts, b. 3 Jan 1881 in Caroline Co, VA, d. 10 Apr 1956; m. 15 Apr 1900 at Shiloh Methodist Church, Bagby, VA, to Richard Lee Southworth, b. 11 Apr 1872, d. 22 Mar 1936. They are buried in Mt Vernon Methodist Church Cemetery, Lorne, VA. Their issue:

1. Carrie Emma Southworth
2. Ella Louise Southworth

Page 132

Carrie Emma Southworth, b. 11 Nov 1904 in Caroline Co, VA, d. 19 Apr 1985 in Richmond, VA, of cardio-pulmonary failure due to thermal burns from a stove fire; m. 2 Jan 1924 to William Claiborne Ancarrow, b. 1894; d. 6 Oct 1979. They are buried in Mt Vernon Methodist Church Cemetery, Lorne, VA. Their issue:

1. William Claiborne (Sonny) Ancarrow Jr
2. Alice Marie Ancarrow
3. Emily Carol Ancarrow

Page 132   William Claiborne (Sonny) Ancarrow Jr, b. 11 May 1925, d. 12 Jun 2012; m. Maegen Quillen, b. 1934, d. 1994. They are buried in Mt Vernon Methodist Church Cemetery, Lorne, VA. Their issue:

1. William Claiborne Ancarrow III
2. Paul Ancarrow
3. Aaron Ancarrow

Page 132   William Claiborne Ancarrow III, b. 1959; m. Theresa __________. Their issue:

1. Megan Ancarrow
2. Brandon Ancarrow
3. Jacob Ancarrow

Page 132   Paul Ancarrow, b. 1963; m. Renee __________

Page 132   Aaron Ancarrow, b. 1966; m. Jennifer __________

Page 132   Alice Marie Ancarrow, b. 21 Sep 1928, m. Edward Franklin Woodall III, b. 5 Sep 1931, d. 27 Jun 2017. Their issue:

1. Mark Robertson Woodall, b. 16 Apr 1957

2.   Eric Barksdale Woodall, b. 18 Apr 1960

3.   John Franklin Woodall, b. 13 Jun 1961; m. Lydia
_____________, b. ____________

Page 132

Emily Carol Ancarrow, b. 9 Nov 1933; m. Forest Brauer, b. 1928, d. 1992. Their issue:

1.   Nancy Carolyn Brauer

2.   Sarah Brauer

3.   Susanne Brauer

Nancy Carolyn Brauer, b. 1958; m. Robert S Tucker, b. 1958

Sarah Brauer, b. 1962; m. Tommy Morris, b. ____________

Susanne Brauer, b. 1964, m. John Scott, b. ____________

Page 132

Ella Louise Southworth, b. 20 Aug 1909 in Caroline Co, VA, d. 30 Apr 1929 in Caroline Co, VA, of conflagration (accidentally); clothes caught on fire when she lit the fire with kerosene; m. Clyde Roseboro Reece, b. 9 Sep 1908, d. 27 Jun 1930. They are buried in Mt Vernon Methodist Church Cemetery, Lorne, VA. Their issue:

1.   Twins, d. at birth

2.   Doris Louise Reece

3.   Clyde Monroe Reece

Page 132

Doris Louise Reece, b. 24 Mar 1927 in Caroline Co, VA, d. 8 Jan 2018; m. 22 May 1948 to Herbert Harrison (Harry) Shelley, b. 1926, d. Jan 2002. They are buried in Mt Vernon Methodist Church Cemetery, Lorne, VA. Their issue:

Susan Ritchie Shelley

Page 132   Susan Ritchie Shelley, b. 11 Nov 1956, m. (1) 11 Jul 1981 in Charlottesville,
VA, to George Ralph Peterson, b. 1 Jan 1949, m. (2) ___________ Burke,
b. ____________. Issue by second marriage:

Allison Louise Burke, b. ____________

Page 132   Clyde Monroe Reece, b. 1928; m. Sarah Bradley. They had three sons
and one daughter.

Page 132   Evelina Pitts, b. 1817 in Caroline Co, VA, d. 1862 at the age of 45

Clifton Farm

Robert Woodford Pitts

Grandpa Pitts

Cinderella Southworth Pitts and Harry Woodford Pitts

THE FAMILY OF FERNANDO PITTS

By His Loving Daughter Bernice Pitts Hudson

My father married my mother's sister. She died, so my father married my mother. My father's youngest brother married my mother's youngest sister. She died, so my father's youngest brother married my mother's oldest sister's daughter. My father's son married my mother's oldest sister's husband's brother's daughter. My father's brother married my mother's father's brother's daughter. My mother's brother may have married my father's sister, but she was killed by lightening.

WHO'S WHO

My father (Fernando) married my mother's sister (Carrie). She died, so my father (Fernando) married my mother (Mollie Kate). My father's (Fernando) youngest brother (Harry) married my mother's (Mollie Kate) youngest sister (Lottie). She died, so my father's (Fernando) youngest brother (Harry) married my mother's (Mollie Kate) oldest sister's (Annie) daughter (Kate). My father's (Fernando) son (Carroll) married my mother's (Mollie Kate) oldest sister's (Annie) husband's (Frank Taylor) brother's (John Taylor) daughter (Ollie). My father's (Fernando) brother (Charlie) married my mother's (Mollie Kate) father's (Edward Barlow) brother's (James Barlow) daughter (Effie). My mother's (Mollie Kate) brother (Joseph) may have married my father's (Fernando) sister (Sabernie), but she was struck and killed by lightening.

NOTE: There is a tombstone in the Mt. Hermon Baptist Church for Sabernie. She was killed in 1900.

The Family of Fernando Pitts

Rose Effie Barlow Pitts & Charles Burton Pitts

Sabernie C Pitts

Harry Woodford Pitts

Family of Harry & Kate Taylor Pitts – 1939

Dolly, Lillian, Ruth & Primp

MARRIAGE ✱ LICENSE

Virginia, Caroline County   to wit:

To any Person Licensed to Celebrate Marriages:

You are hereby authorized to join together in the Holy State of Matrimony, according to the rites and ceremonies of your Church, or religious denomination, and the laws of the Commonwealth of Virginia,

Fernando H Pitts

and Carrie Barlow,

Given under my hand, as Clerk of the County Court of Caroline this 24th day of Dec, 1894.

E. R. Coghill Clerk.

CERTIFICATE TO OBTAIN A MARRIAGE LICENSE,
TO BE ANNEXED TO THE LICENSE, REQUIRED BY SECTION 2229 OF THE CODE OF VIRGINIA.

Time of Marriage, Dec 26th 1894	Place of Husband's Birth, Caroline Co. Va.
Place of Marriage, Mt Hermon Church	Place of Wife's Birth, " " "
Full Names of Parties Married, As above	Place of Husband's Residence, " " "
	Place of Wife's Residence, " " "
Color, White	Names of Husband's Parents, Robert and Lucinda Pitts
Age of Husband, 21 years	
Age of Wife, 21 "	Names of Wife's Parents, Edward D. and Rosa B. Barlow
Condition of Husband (widowed or single),	
Condition of Wife (widowed or single),	Occupation of Husband, Farmer

Given under my hand this 24 day of Dec 1894.

E. R. Coghill Clerk.

MINISTER'S RETURN OF MARRIAGE.

I Certify, That on the 26th day of December 1894 at Mt Hermon Church I united in Marriage the above-named and described parties, under authority of the annexed License.

E. W. McCown.

The Minister celebrating a marriage, is required, within TEN days thereafter, to return the license to the Office of the Clerk who issued the same, with an endorsement thereon of the FACT of such marriage, and of the TIME and PLACE of celebrating the same.

Marriage License of Fernando H Pitts & Carrie Barlow.

MARRIAGE ✳ LICENSE

Virginia, Caroline County   to wit:

To any Person Licensed to Celebrate Marriages:

You are hereby authorized to join together in the Holy State of Matrimony, according to the rites and ceremonies of your Church, or religious denomination, and the laws of the Commonwealth of Virginia,

Charles B. Pitts

and   Rose Effie Barlow

Given under my hand, as Clerk of the   Circuit   Court of   Caroline   this   9th   day of February   1904.

E. R. Coghill   Clerk.

CERTIFICATE TO OBTAIN A MARRIAGE LICENSE,
TO BE ANNEXED TO THE LICENSE, REQUIRED BY SECTION 2225 OF THE CODE OF VIRGINIA AS AMENDED BY ACT OF FEBRUARY 2, 1900.

Time of Marriage, February 10, 1904	Place of Husband's Birth, Caroline Co. Va.
Place of Marriage, Mt. Hermon Ch. Caroline Co.	Place of Wife's Birth, " " "
Full Names of Parties Married,	Place of Husband's Residence, " " "
(as above)	Place of Wife's Residence, " " "
Color, white	Names of Husband's Parents, Robert & Lucinda
Age of Husband, 26 years	Pitts
Age of Wife, 22 "	Names of Wife's Parents, James and
Condition of Husband (widowed or single or divorced)	Bettie Barlow
Condition of Wife (widowed or single or divorced)	Occupation of Husband, Farmer

Given under my hand this   9th   day of February   1904.

E. R. Coghill   Clerk.

Certificate of Time and Place of Marriage.

I, Andrew Broaddus, a Minister of the Baptist — Church, or religious order of that name, do certify that on the 10th — day of Feb — 1904, at Mt. Hermon Church, under authority of the above License, I united in Marriage the persons named and described therein.

Given under my hand this   15th   day of Feb — 1904. –

Andrew Broaddus. —

☞ The Minister celebrating a marriage is required, within two months thereafter, to return the License to the Office of the Clerk who issued the same, with an endorsement thereon of the FACT of such marriage, and of the TIME and PLACE of celebrating the same.

Marriage License of Charles B Pitts & Rose Effie Barlow

MARRIAGE LICENSE

Virginia, *Caroline County* to wit:

To any Person Licensed to Celebrate Marriages:

You are hereby authorized to join together in the Holy State of Matrimony, according to the rites and ceremonies of your Church, or religious denomination, and the laws of the Commonwealth of Virginia,

Harry Woodford Pitts

and *Laura Meade Barlow*

Given under my hand, as Clerk of the *Circuit* Court of *Caroline* this *16* day of *March* *1907*.

E. R. Coghill Clerk.

CERTIFICATE TO OBTAIN A MARRIAGE LICENSE.

TO BE ANNEXED TO THIS LICENSE, REQUIRED BY SECTION 2230 OF THE CODE OF VIRGINIA, AS AMENDED BY ACT OF FEBRUARY 3, 1900.

Time of Marriage, *March 17, 1907*

Place of Marriage, *Caroline Co. Va.*

Full Names of Parties Married, *us about*

Color, *White*

Age of Husband, *25 Years (over age)*

Age of Wife, *20*

Condition of Husband (widowed or single or divorced)

Condition of Wife (widowed or single or divorced)

Place of Husband's Birth, *Caroline Co. Va.*

Place of Wife's Birth, *" " "*

Place of Husband's Residence, *" " "*

Place of Wife's Residence, *" " "*

Names of Husband's Parents, *Robert and Silverite Pitts*

Names of Wife's Parents, *Edwd. B. and Rose Bell Barlow.*

Occupation of Husband, *Farmer*

Given under my hand this *16* day of *March* *1907*

E. R. Coghill Clerk.

Certificate of Time and Place of Marriage.

I, *Joseph F. Billingsley*, a Minister of the *Baptist* Church, or religious order of that name, do certify that on the *17* day of *March* *1907*, at *House of Parents*, under authority of the above License, I united in Marriage the persons named and described therein.

Given under my hand this *18* day of *March* *1907*.

Joseph F. Billingsley

The Minister celebrating a marriage is required, within two months thereafter, to return the License to the Office of the Clerk who issued the same, with an endorsement thereon of the FACT of such marriage, and of the TIME and PLACE of celebrating the same.

Marriage License of Harry Woodford Pitts & Laura Meade Barlow

MARRIAGE LICENSE

Virginia, _Caroline County_ to wit:

To any Person Licensed to Celebrate Marriages:

You are hereby authorized to join together in the Holy State of Matrimony according to the rites and ceremonies of your Church, or religious denomination, and the laws of the Commonwealth of Virginia,

Robert Pitts

and _Sallie Covington_

Given under my hand, as Clerk of the _County_ Court of _Caroline_ this _26th_ day of _August_ 19_03_

E. R. Coghill _Clerk._

CERTIFICATE TO OBTAIN A MARRIAGE LICENSE

TO BE ANNEXED TO THE LICENSE, REQUIRED BY SECTION 2229 OF THE CODE OF VIRGINIA AS AMENDED BY ACT OF FEBRUARY 3, 1900.

Time of Marriage, _August 26. 1903._ | Place of Husband's Birth, _Caroline Co. Va._

Place of Marriage, _Bowling Green Caroline Co. Va._ | Place of Wife's Birth, " "

Full Names of Parties Married, | Place of Husband's Residence, " " "

as above | Place of Wife's Residence, " " "

Color, _White_ | Names of Husband's Parents, _George and_

Age of Husband, _44 years_ | _Bettie Pitts_

Age of Wife, _17 "_ | Name of Wife's Parents, _Albert and_

Condition of Husband ~~widowed or~~ single ~~or divorced~~ | _Luvinia Covington_

Condition of Wife ~~widowed or~~ single ~~or divorced~~ | Occupation of Husband, _Farmer._

Given under my hand this _26._ day of _August_ 19_03._

E. R. Coghill _Clerk_

Certificate of Time and Place of Marriage.

I _E. L. Peerman_, a minister of the _M. E. Church, South._ Church, or religious order of that name, do certify that on the _twenty sixth_ day of _August_ 1903, at _Bowling Green_, under authority of the above License, I united in Marriage the persons named and described therein. Given under my hand this _26th_ day of _August_ 1903.

E. L. Peerman

The Minister Celebrating a marriage is required within two months thereafter, to return the License to the Office of the Clerk who issued the same, with an endorsement thereon of the FACT of such marriage, and of the TIME and PLACE of celebrating the same.

Marriage License of Robert Pitts & Sallie Covington

CERTIFICATION OF VITAL RECORD

COMMONWEALTH OF VIRGINIA

DEPARTMENT OF HEALTH - DIVISION OF VITAL RECORDS

Registration District No. 160 B 0160   Registered No. 33

CERTIFICATE OF DEATH
COMMONWEALTH OF VIRGINIA
DEPARTMENT OF HEALTH, BUREAU OF VITAL STATISTICS   27022

1. PLACE OF DEATH
a. COUNTY Caroline
b. MAGISTERIAL DISTRICT Bowling Green
c. CITY OR TOWN Kidds Fork
d. IS PLACE OF DEATH INSIDE CITY LIMITS? YES ☐ NO ☒
e. HOSPITAL OR INSTITUTION None
f. LENGTH OF STAY

2. USUAL RESIDENCE (Where deceased lived. If institution: residence before admission)
a. STATE Va.
b. COUNTY Caroline
c. CITY OR TOWN Kidds Fork
d. IS RESIDENCE INSIDE CITY LIMITS? YES ☐ NO ☒
e. STREET ADDRESS (If rural, give mailing address) None
f. IS RESIDENCE ON A FARM? YES ☒ NO ☐

3. NAME OF DECEASED (Type or Print) a. (First) HARRY b. (Middle) WOODFORD c. (Last) PITTS

4. DATE OF DEATH (Month) (Day) (Year) Nov. 9, 1955

5. SEX Male
6. COLOR OR RACE White
7. MARRIED ☒ NEVER MARRIED ☐ WIDOWED ☐ DIVORCED ☐
8. DATE OF BIRTH Nov. 27, 1881
9. AGE (In years last birthday) 74   IF UNDER 1 YR. Months Days   IF UNDER 24 HRS. Hours Min.

10a. USUAL OCCUPATION (Give kind of work done during most of working life, even if retired) Farmer
10b. KIND OF BUSINESS OR INDUSTRY Farm Owner
11. BIRTHPLACE (State or foreign country) Va.
12. CITIZEN OF WHAT COUNTRY? US

13. FATHER'S NAME Robert W. Pitts
14. MOTHER'S MAIDEN NAME Cinderella Pitts

15. NAME OF HUSBAND OR WIFE OF DECEASED Annie Taylor Pitts
16. SOCIAL SECURITY NO.
17. INFORMANT'S SIGNATURE X Mrs. Harry Pitts ADDRESS Kidds Fork, Va.

18. CAUSE OF DEATH (Enter only one cause per line for (a), (b), and (c).)
PART I. DEATH WAS CAUSED BY:
IMMEDIATE CAUSE (a) Paralysis Agitans
Conditions, if any, which gave rise to above cause (a), stating the underlying cause last. DUE TO (b) Arteriosclerosis
DUE TO (c)
INTERVAL BETWEEN ONSET AND DEATH

PART II. OTHER SIGNIFICANT CONDITIONS CONTRIBUTING TO DEATH BUT NOT RELATED TO THE TERMINAL DISEASE CONDITION GIVEN IN PART I(a)

19. WAS AUTOPSY PERFORMED? YES ☐ NO ☒

20a. ACCIDENT ☐ SUICIDE ☐ HOMICIDE ☐
20b. DESCRIBE HOW INJURY OCCURRED. (Enter nature of injury in Part I or Part II of item 18.)
20c. TIME OF INJURY Hour a.m. p.m. Month, Day, Year
20d. INJURY OCCURRED WHILE AT WORK ☐ NOT WHILE AT WORK ☐
20e. PLACE OF INJURY (e.g., in or about home, farm, factory, street, office bldg., etc.)
20f. CITY, TOWN, OR LOCATION   COUNTY   STATE

21. I attended the deceased from August 1951, to Nov. 9, 1956 and last saw him alive on Oct. 31, 1956
Death occurred at 7 P. m on the date stated above; and to the best of my knowledge, from the causes stated.
22a. SIGNATURE George A. Reynolds MD
22b. ADDRESS Bowling Green
22c. DATE SIGNED 11/12/56

23a. BURIAL, CREMATION, REMOVAL (Specify) Burial
23b. DATE Nov. 11, 1956
23c. NAME OF CEMETERY OR CREMATORY Mt. Hermon Baptist Cemetery
23d. LOCATION (City, town, or county) (State) Shumansville, Va.
DATE REC'D BY LOCAL REG. 11-17-56
REGISTRAR'S SIGNATURE
24. FUNERAL DIRECTOR'S SIGNATURE W. L. Hoy
ADDRESS Manna-Hoy Funeral Home Bowling Green, Va.

This is to certify that this is a true and correct reproduction or abstract of the official record filed with the Virginia Department of Health, Richmond, Virginia.

DATE ISSUED

AUG 0 4 1994

Russell E. Booker, Jr.
Russell E. Booker, Jr., State Registrar

Any reproduction of this document is prohibited by statute. Do not accept unless on security paper with seal of Vital Statistics clearly embossed. Section 32.1-272, Code of Virginia, as amended.

VS 15B

ANY ALTERATION OR ERASURE VOIDS THIS CERTIFICATE

Certificate of Death for Harry Woodford Pitts

CERTIFICATION OF VITAL RECORD

COMMONWEALTH OF VIRGINIA

DEPARTMENT OF HEALTH - DIVISION OF VITAL RECORDS

COMMONWEALTH OF VIRGINIA — CERTIFICATE OF DEATH

DEPARTMENT OF HEALTH — BUREAU OF VITAL RECORDS AND HEALTH STATISTICS — RICHMOND

COPY A
FOR BUREAU OF VITAL STATISTICS

REGISTRATION AREA NUMBER **143** CERTIFICATE NUMBER **156** STATE FILE NUMBER **74-005851**

DECEDENT

1. FULL NAME OF DECEASED — (first) Annie (middle) Taylor (last) Pitts
2. SEX — male ☐ female ☒
3. DATE OF DEATH (mo.) (day) (year) — February 17 1974
4. AGE OF DECEASED — 76 years / IF UNDER 1 YEAR months days / IF UNDER 1 DAY hours minutes
5. COLOR OR RACE — White

PLACE OF DEATH

6. NAME OF HOSPITAL OR INSTITUTION OF DEATH (if none, so state)
7. COUNTY OF DEATH (if independent city, leave blank) — Henrico
8. CITY OR TOWN OF DEATH (if rural, so state) — Richmond / inside city or town limits? yes ☐ no ☒
9. STREET ADDRESS OR RT. NO. OF PLACE OF DEATH — 7511 Moss Side Ave.

USUAL RESIDENCE OF DECEDENT

10. STATE (OR FOREIGN COUNTRY) OF DECEASED'S RESIDENCE — Virginia
11. COUNTY OF DECEASED'S RESIDENCE (if independent city, leave blank) — Caroline
12. CITY OR TOWN OF RESIDENCE — Milford / inside city or town limits? yes ☐ no ☒
13. STREET ADDRESS OR RT. NO. OF RESIDENCE — RFD
ZIP CODE — 22514

PERSONAL DATA OF DECEDENT

14. NAME OF FATHER OF DECEASED — Frank L. Taylor
15. MAIDEN NAME OF MOTHER OF DECEASED — Annie Belle Barlow
16. DECEASED CITIZEN OF WHAT COUNTRY — USA
17. MARRIED ☐ NEVER MARRIED ☐ WIDOWED ☒ DIVORCED ☐
18. IF MARRIED OR WIDOWED, NAME OF SPOUSE — Harry Woodford Pitts
19. SOCIAL SECURITY NUMBER — 229-52-9808
20. IF VETERAN, name war, or if peacetime only, so state
21. BIRTHPLACE OF DECEASED (state or country) — Virginia
22. DATE OF BIRTH (mo.) (day) (year) OF DECEASED — Aug. 4, 1897
23. USUAL OR LAST OCCUPATION — Homemaker
24. KIND OF BUSINESS OR INDUSTRY
25. INFORMANT — OR SOURCE OF INFORMATION — Family

TO PHYSICIAN:

26. CAUSE OF DEATH (Enter only one cause per line for (A), (B), and (C).
PART I. DEATH WAS CAUSED BY:
IMMEDIATE CAUSE (A) Cerebral damage — INTERVAL BETWEEN ONSET AND DEATH — 10 yrs
DUE TO
Conditions, if any, which gave rise to immediate cause (A), stating the underlying cause last. (B) ______ DUE TO
(C) ______

PART II. OTHER SIGNIFICANT CONDITIONS CONTRIBUTING TO DEATH BUT NOT RELATED TO THE TERMINAL DISEASE CONDITION GIVEN IN PART I (A)
26a. AUTOPSY? yes ☐ no ☐ AUTHORIZED BY:

26b. IF FEMALE, WAS THERE A PREGNANCY IN PAST 3 MONTHS? yes ☐ no ☐ unknown ☐
26c. IF EXTERNAL CAUSE, IT WAS PRIMARY ☐ or CONTRIBUTING ☐ TO CAUSE OF DEATH. NOTE: IF EXTERNAL CAUSE, NOTIFY MED. EXAMINER
26d. DESCRIBE HOW INJURY OCCURRED. (enter nature of injury in part I or part II)
26e. TIME OF INJURY (mo.) (day) (year) A.M. P.M.
26f. INJURY OCCURRED while at work ☐ not while at work ☐
26g. PLACE OF INJURY (home, farm, factory, street, office bldg., etc.)
26h. (city or town) (county) (state)

26i. I CERTIFY that I attended the deceased from (date) 29 Sept 71 to 17 Feb 74 and that death occurred at 12:30 AM ☐ PM ☐ from the cause stated above
ACTUAL SIGNATURE ▶ Herbert G Ruffin M.D.
ADDRESS: (CITY AND STATE) — Richmond Va
DATE SIGNED: 2-27-74

FUNERAL DIRECTOR

27. BURIAL ☒ REMOVAL ☐ CREMATION ☐
28. PLACE OF BURIAL, REMOVAL, ETC. (name of cemetery or crematory) Mt. Hermon Bapt. Church, Caroline Co. (city or county) Virginia (state)
29. (signature of funeral director or person acting as such) Paul W Manns
NAME OF FUNERAL HOME AND ADDRESS — Manns Funeral Home, Bowling Green, Va. 22427
30. (signature of registrar) Joan Huly Pitts — Deputy REGISTRAR
DATE RECORD FILED — FEB 27 1974

VS2 3-70

This is to certify that this is a true and correct reproduction or abstract of the official record filed with the Virginia Department of Health, Richmond, Virginia.

DATE ISSUED **AUG 0 4 1994**

Russell E. Booker, Jr., State Registrar

Certificate of Death for Annie Taylor Pitts

CERTIFICATE OF DEATH

Form No. 12.

COMMONWEALTH OF VIRGINIA
Bureau of Vital Statistics
State Board of Health

File No.—For State Registrar Only
18242

1. PLACE OF DEATH.

County of _Caroline_

District of _Reedy Church_
or
Inc. Town of _Bagby P.O._
or
City of __________

Registration District No. _160_

(No. __________ St.; __________ Ward)

Registered No. _12_
(Name of Local Registrar)

[If death occurred in a Hospital or Institution give its NAME instead of street and number.]

2. FULL NAME _Norburn Pitts Jr_

Residence
In City ___ Yrs. ___ Mos. ___ Days ___

PERSONAL AND STATISTICAL PARTICULARS	MEDICAL CERTIFICATE OF DEATH

PERSONAL AND STATISTICAL PARTICULARS

3 SEX _Male_

4 COLOR OR RACE _White_

5 SINGLE, MARRIED, WIDOWED, OR DIVORCED. (Write the word) _Married_

6 DATE OF BIRTH
(Month) __________ (Day) _1_ (Year) __________

7 AGE _66_ yrs. ___ mos. ___ ds. If LESS than 1 day, ___ hrs. or ___ min.?

8 OCCUPATION
(a) Trade, profession, or particular kind of work _Farmer_
(b) General nature of Industry, business, or establishment in which employed (or employer)

9 BIRTHPLACE (State or Country) _Caroline Co. Va.,_

10 NAME OF FATHER _Norburn Pitts_

11 BIRTHPLACE OF FATHER (State or Country) _Caroline Co. Va.,_

12 MAIDEN NAME OF MOTHER _Malinda Moran_

13 BIRTHPLACE OF MOTHER (State or Country) _Virginia_

14 THE ABOVE IS TRUE TO THE BEST OF MY KNOWLEDGE

(Informant) _Willis Pitts_

(Address) _Bagby Va,_

Filed _July 2_, 191_9_. _Mrs. L. M. Head_
LOCAL REGISTRAR

MEDICAL CERTIFICATE OF DEATH

16 DATE OF DEATH _July_ (Month) _1_ (Day), _1919_ (Year)

17 I HEREBY CERTIFY, That I attended deceased from _April 28_ 191_9_, to _June 30_, 191_9_ that I last saw him alive on _June 30_, 191_9_ and that death occurred, on the date stated above, at _3 a._ m.

The CAUSE OF DEATH* was as follows:
Epileptic convulsion

(Duration) ___ yrs. ___ mos. ___ ds.

Contributory (SECONDARY) _Weakened heart action_
(Duration) ___ yrs. _2_ mos. ___ ds.

(Signed) _L. J. Head_ M. D.
July 1, 191_9_ (Address) _Penola Va_

*State the DISEASE CAUSING DEATH, or, in deaths from VIOLENT CAUSES, state (1) MEANS OF INJURY; and (2) whether ACCIDENTAL, SUICIDAL or HOMICIDAL.

18 LENGTH OF RESIDENCE (For Hospitals, Institutions, Transients, or recent Residents
At place of death ___ yrs. ___ mos. ___ ds. In the State ___ yrs. ___ mos. ___ ds.
Where was disease contracted, if not at place of death? __________
Former or usual Residence __________

19 PLACE OF BURIAL OR REMOVAL. _At home_

DATE OF BURIAL __________, 191___

20 UNDERTAKER _Family_

ADDRESS _Bagby_

MARGIN RESERVED FOR BINDING

WRITE PLAINLY WITH UNFADING BLACK INK—THIS IS A PERMANENT RECORD.

N. B.—Every item of Information should be carefully supplied. AGE should be stated EXACTLY. PHYSICIANS should state CAUSE OF DEATH in plain terms, so that it may be properly classified. Exact statement of OCCUPATION is very important. See Instructions on back of certificate.

Certificate of Death for Norburn Pitts Jr.

CERTIFICATE OF DEATH
COMMONWEALTH OF VIRGINIA
DEPARTMENT OF HEALTH
BUREAU OF VITAL STATISTICS

29281

1 PLACE OF DEATH
COUNTY OF *Montgomery*
MAGISTERIAL DISTRICT OF *Blacksburg*
OR INC. TOWN OF ____
OR CITY OF ____

REGISTRATION DISTRICT No. *602-B*   REGISTERED No. *45*
(TO BE INSERTED BY REGISTRAR)   (FOR USE OF LOCAL REGISTRAR)

(No. ________ St. ________ Ward)
(If death occurred in a hospital or other institution, give its NAME instead of street and number)

Length of residence in city or town where death occurred ____ yrs. *4* mos. *1* ds. ____ How long in U. S., if of foreign birth? ____ yrs. ____ mos. ____ ds

2 FULL NAME *Hampton Pitts*

(A) RESIDENCE. No. *Montgomery Camp, Blacksburg* WARD
(Usual place of abode)   (If nonresident give city or town and State)

PERSONAL AND STATISTICAL PARTICULARS

3. SEX *M*

4. COLOR OR RACE *W*

5. SINGLE, MARRIED, WIDOWED, OR DIVORCED (write the word) *W.*

5A. IF MARRIED, WIDOWED, OR DIVORCED HUSBAND OF (OR) WIFE OF *Not Known*

6. DATE OF BIRTH (month, day, and year) *1899*

7. AGE   Years *36*   Months *8*   Days *10*   IF LESS THAN 1 DAY, ____ HRS. OR ____ MIN.

OCCUPATION
8. TRADE, PROFESSION, OR PARTICULAR KIND OF WORK DONE, AS SPINNER, SAWYER, BOOKKEEPER, ETC. ____

9. INDUSTRY OR BUSINESS IN WHICH WORK WAS DONE. AS SILK MILL, SAW MILL, BANK, ETC. ____

10. DATE DECEASED LAST WORKED AT THIS OCCUPATION (month and year) ____   11. TOTAL TIME (YEARS) SPENT IN THIS OCCUPATION ____

12. BIRTHPLACE (city or town) (State or country) ____

FATHER
13. NAME ____
14. BIRTHPLACE (city or town) (State or country) ____

MOTHER
15. MAIDEN NAME ____
16. BIRTHPLACE (city or town) (State or country) ____

17. INFORMANT *J. C. F. Flanagan*
(ADDRESS) *Blacksburg Va*

18. BURIAL, CREMATION, OR REMOVAL
PLACE *Christiansburg*   *Dec 28 1935*

19. UNDERTAKER *Jos. Richardson*
(ADDRESS) *Christiansburg*

20. FILED *Dec 31 1935*   *Julia E. Price* Registrar

MEDICAL CERTIFICATE OF DEATH

21. DATE OF DEATH (month, day, and year) *Dec. 25 1935*

22. I HEREBY CERTIFY, That I attended deceased from *Aug 24*, 19*35* To *Dec 25*, 19*35*
I LAST SAW HIM ALIVE ON *Dec 25*, 19*35*. DEATH IS SAID TO HAVE OCCURRED ON THE DATE STATED ABOVE, AT *12:20 P* M.
THE PRINCIPAL CAUSE OF DEATH AND RELATED CAUSES OF IMPORTANCE IN ORDER OF ONSET WERE AS FOLLOWS:

Date of onset

Pulmonary Tuberculosis   *years*

CONTRIBUTORY CAUSES OF IMPORTANCE NOT RELATED TO PRINCIPAL CAUSE:

NAME OF OPERATION ____ DATE OF ____

WHAT TEST CONFIRMED DIAGNOSIS? ____ WAS THERE AN AUTOPSY? *No*

23. IF DEATH WAS DUE TO EXTERNAL CAUSES (VIOLENCE) FILL IN ALSO THE FOLLOWING:
ACCIDENT, SUICIDE, OR HOMICIDE? ____ DATE OF INJURY ____
WHERE DID INJURY OCCUR? ____ (Specify city or town, county, and State)
SPECIFY WHETHER INJURY OCCURRED IN INDUSTRY, IN HOME, OR IN PUBLIC PLACE. ____
MANNER OF INJURY ____
NATURE OF INJURY ____

24. WAS DISEASE OR INJURY IN ANY WAY RELATED TO OCCUPATION OF DECEASED? *No*
IF SO, SPECIFY ____

(SIGNED) *J. E. K. Flanagan* M. D.
(ADDRESS) *Montgomery Camp, Blacksburg*

Certificate of Death for Hampton Pitts

COMMONWEALTH OF VIRGINIA—CERTIFICATE OF DEATH

DEPARTMENT OF HEALTH—BUREAU OF VITAL RECORDS AND HEALTH STATISTICS—RICHMOND

COPY A

FOR BUREAU OF VITAL STATISTICS

REGISTRATION AREA NUMBER **222** CERTIFICATE NUMBER **1312**

MEDICAL EXAMINER'S CERTIFICATE

STATE FILE NUMBER **85-014606**

DECEDENT

1. FULL NAME OF DECEASED (first) (middle) (last): CARRIE EMMA ANCARROW
2. SEX: female ☒
3. RACE: WHITE
4. DATE OF DEATH (mo.) (day) (year): APRIL 19, 1985
5. AGE: 80 years
6. DATE OF BIRTH (mo.) (day) (year): NOV 11, 1904
7. WAS DECEDENT EVER IN U.S. ARMED FORCES? no ☒

PLACE OF DEATH

8. NAME OF HOSPITAL OR INSTITUTION OF DEATH (if none, so state): MEDICAL COLLEGE OF VA — Inpatient ☒
9. COUNTY OF DEATH (if independent city, leave blank):
10. CITY OR TOWN OF DEATH: RICHMOND, VA. — inside city or town limits? yes ☒
11. STREET ADDRESS OR RT. NO. OF PLACE OF DEATH: 401 NORTH 12TH STREET

USUAL RESIDENCE OF DECEDENT

12. STATE (OR FOREIGN COUNTRY) OF DECEASED'S RESIDENCE: VIRGINIA
13. COUNTY OF DECEASED'S RESIDENCE (if independent city, leave blank): CAROLINE
14. CITY OR TOWN OF RESIDENCE: RUTHER GLEN — inside city or town limits? no ☒
15. STREET ADDRESS OR RT. NO. OF RESIDENCE: ROUTE 3, BOX 216
ZIP CODE: 22546

PERSONAL DATA OF DECEDENT

16. NAME OF FATHER OF DECEASED: RICHARD LEE SOUTHWORTH
17. MAIDEN NAME OF MOTHER OF DECEASED: NANNIE PITTS
18. CITIZEN OF WHAT COUNTRY: U.S.A.
19. BIRTHPLACE (state or country): VIRGINIA
20. NEVER MARRIED / DIVORCED / MARRIED / WIDOWED ☒
21. IF MARRIED OR WIDOWED, NAME OF SPOUSE (if divorced leave blank): WILLIAM CLAIBORNE ANCARROW
23. USUAL OR LAST OCCUPATION: HOMEMAKER
24. KIND OF BUSINESS OR INDUSTRY:
25. INFORMANT - OR SOURCE OF INFORMATION: EMILY A. BRAUER

TO MEDICAL EXAMINER:

26. CAUSE OF DEATH (Enter only one cause per line for (A), (B), and (C).)

PART I. DEATH WAS CAUSED BY:

IMMEDIATE CAUSE (A): Sepsis and Cardiopulmonary Failure — INTERVAL BETWEEN ONSET AND DEATH: days

DUE TO (B): Thermal Burns — days

Conditions, if any, which gave rise to immediate cause (A), stating the underlying cause last.

DUE TO (C): Stove Fire — days

PART II. OTHER SIGNIFICANT CONDITIONS CONTRIBUTING TO DEATH BUT NOT RELATED TO THE TERMINAL DISEASE CONDITION GIVEN IN PART I (A)

26J. AUTOPSY? AUTHORIZED BY: no ☒

26b. IF FEMALE, WAS THERE A PREGNANCY IN PAST 3 MONTHS? unknown ☒

26c. IF EXTERNAL CAUSE, IT WAS PRIMARY ☒ or CONTRIBUTING TO CAUSE OF DEATH

26d. DESCRIBE HOW INJURY RELATING TO DEATH OCCURRED: victims clothing caught fire when she leaned against stove at home

26e. TIME OF INJURY (mo.) (day) (year): 1:00 AM APRIL 10, 1985

26f. INJURY OCCURRED: not while at work ☒

26g. PLACE OF INJURY (home, farm, factory, street, office bldg., etc.): home

26h. (city or town) (county) (state): RUTHER GLEN, VA.

26I. I CERTIFY that I took charge of the remains described above, viewed the body, made inquiry and in my opinion death resulted at or about 08:20 (PM) from:

NATURAL CAUSES ☐ ACCIDENT ☒ SUICIDE ☐ HOMICIDE ☐ UNDETERMINED ☐ PENDING ☐

ACTUAL SIGNATURE ▶ *Jack W. Snyder, MD*

DATE SIGNED: 19 April 1985

NAME OF MEDICAL EXAMINER (Type or print): JACK W. SNYDER, M.D.
ADDRESS OF MEDICAL EXAMINER: 9 N. 14th Street

NOTE! If "Pending" must be indicated, notify registrar of final decision as soon as possible.

FUNERAL DIRECTOR

27. BURIAL ☒ REMOVAL ☐ CREMATION ☐
28. PLACE OF BURIAL, REMOVAL, ETC. (name of cemetery or crematory): MT. VERNON METHODIST CHURCH, (city or county) RUTHER GLEN, (state) VIRGINIA
29. (Signature of funeral director or person legally filing this certificate): *Stewart F. Reid*
NAME OF FUNERAL HOME AND ADDRESS: REID FUNERAL HOME, INC. P.O. BOX 930, ASHLAND, VIRGINIA

REGISTRAR

30. (Signature of registrar): *L. N. Andrews*
DATE RECORD FILED: 4-24-85

VS 2A 12/79

Certificate of Death for Carrie Emma Ancarrow

CERTIFICATE OF DEATH
COMMONWEALTH OF VIRGINIA
BUREAU OF VITAL STATISTICS
STATE BOARD OF HEALTH

FORM NO. 15

10978

1 PLACE OF DEATH

COUNTY OF *Henrico*

MAGISTERIAL DISTRICT OF

OR INC. TOWN OF

OR CITY OF *Richmond*

REGISTRATION DISTRICT NO. ______ (TO BE INSERTED BY REGISTRAR)

REGISTERED NO. **1117** (FOR USE OF LOCAL REGISTRAR)

(No. *St. Luke's Hospital* ST. ______ WARD)
(If death occured in a hospital or other institution, give its NAME instead of street and number)

2 FULL NAME *Mrs. Ella Southward Reece*

(A) RESIDENCE. NO. *Point Eastern Va* ST. ______ WARD *Point Eastern, Va.*
(Usual place of abode) (If non-resident give city or town and State)

Length of residence in city or town where death occured ______ yrs. ______ mos. ______ ds. How long in U. S., if of foreign birth? ______ yrs. ______ mos. ______ ds.

PERSONAL AND STATISTICAL PARTICULARS

3 SEX *Female*

4 COLOR OR RACE *White*

5 SINGLE, MARRIED, WIDOWED, OR DIVORCED (write the word) *Married*

5A IF MARRIED, WIDOWED, OR DIVORCED HUSBAND OF (OR) WIFE OF *C. R. Reese*

6 DATE OF BIRTH (MONTH, DAY, AND YEAR, WRITE NAME OF MONTH) *Aug 20 1909* 19__

7 AGE — YEARS *19* — MONTHS *8* — DAYS *10* — IF LESS THAN 1 DAY, ___ HRS OR ___ MIN.

8 OCCUPATION OF DECEASED
(A) TRADE, PROFESSION, OR PARTICULAR KIND OF WORK *At Home*
(B) GENERAL NATURE OF INDUSTRY, BUSINESS, OR ESTABLISHMENT IN WHICH EMPLOYED (OR EMPLOYER)
(C) NAME OF EMPLOYER

9 BIRTHPLACE (CITY OR TOWN) *Caroline Co*
(STATE OR COUNTRY) *Va*

10 NAME OF FATHER *P. L. Southworth*

11 BIRTHPLACE OF FATHER (CITY OR TOWN) *Caroline Co*
(STATE OR COUNTRY) *Va*

12 MAIDEN NAME OF MOTHER *Nanny Pitts*

13 BIRTHPLACE OF MOTHER (CITY OR TOWN)
(STATE OR COUNTRY) *Va*

14 INFORMANT *C. R. Reese*
(ADDRESS) *Point Eastern Va*

15 FILED *5/1* 19*29* *W B Foster* REGISTRAR

MEDICAL CERTIFICATE OF DEATH

16 DATE OF DEATH (MONTH, DAY, AND YEAR. WRITE NAME OF MONTH) *April 20* 19*29*

17 I HEREBY CERTIFY, THAT I ATTENDED DECEASED FROM *Jan 25* 19*29* TO *April 30* 19*29*

THAT I LAST SAW HER ALIVE ON *April 30, 19 29*

AND THAT DEATH OCCURED, ON DATE STATED ABOVE, AT *7* P. M.

THE CAUSE OF DEATH* WAS AS FOLLOWS:

Conflagration —
accidental.
Clothes caught fire
while she was lit. ...

(DURATION) ______ YRS. ______ MOS. ______ DS.

CONTRIBUTORY

(DURATION) ______ YRS. ______ MOS. ______ DS.

18 WHERE WAS DISEASE CONTRACTED IF NOT AT PLACE OF DEATH?

DID AN OPERATION PRECEDE DEATH? *No* DATE OF ______

WAS THERE AN AUTOPSY? *No*

WHAT TEST CONFIRMED DIAGNOSIS?

(SIGNED) *W R Southward* M. D.

4/30, 19*29* (ADDRESS) *St Luke's Hosp.*

*State the DISEASE CAUSING DEATH, or in deaths from VIOLENT CAUSES, state (1) MEANS AND NATURE OF INJURY, and (2) whether ACCIDENTAL, SUICIDAL, or HOMICIDAL.

19 PLACE OF BURIAL, CREMATION, OR REMOVAL *Caroline Co, Va*

DATE OF BURIAL *5/1/1929*

20 UNDERTAKER *Henry Th Woody*
ADDRESS *City*

Certificate of Death for Ella Southward Reece.

FAMILY WORSHIP

Father would reach upon the shelf
And take the Bible down,
In his armchair he'd seat himself,
Then call his flock around.

He'd read some verses from the Book,
In his reverent way,
When from its food our souls partook,
He'd say, "Now, let us pray."

We all would kneel together there,
Our cares would disappear,
The earnestness of father's prayer
Would tell us God was near.

We'd rise and going off to bed,
To rest throughout the night,
Content whatever lay ahead,
His grace would ease our plight.

This is the way that it should be,
In homes where loved ones dwell,
The love God holds for you and me
We daily should retell.

When families are taught to pray
In bright or dreary weather,
You can bet your bottom dollar they
Will always stay together.

THE SOUTHWORTH FAMILY CORRECTIONS & ADDITIONAL INFORMATION

Page 265   William Southworth, b. 1690, d. ___________; m. to Catherine
Nash, b. 1691, d. ___________. Their issue:

1.   Elizabeth Southworth, b. 1728
2.   William Southworth II, b. 1730

William Southworth II, b. 1730 in Middlesex Co, VA, d. 1802; m.
Jane Burk(e), b. 1736, d. 1808. Their issue:

1.   James B Southworth
2.   Robert Southworth, b. 1770, d. 1843
3.   John W Southworth, b. 1773, d. 1870

James B. Southworth, b. 1765 in Caroline Co, VA, d. 1845 in
Franklin Co, MO; m. in 1785 to Agnes Anne Burnett, b. 1765, d.
1815 in Caroline Co, VA. James is buried in Japan (Franklin Co),
MO. Their issue:

1.   Jane B Southworth, b. 1802, d. 1880
2.   James Burnett Southworth
3,   John Achilles Southworth

4.   Elizabeth Ann Southworth, b. c. 1804, d. __________

5.   William H Southworth, b. c .1810, d. 1874

James Burnett Southworth, b. 1806 in Buckingham Co, VA, d. 26 Feb 1864 in Josephine Co, OR. In 1836 he was living in Franklin Co, MO, where he m. (1) 23 Jul 1836 to Exony Reeves, b. 1818, d. 1849 in Franklin Co, MO; m. (2) 13 Jun 1850 in Franklin Co, MO, to Catherine Bridgett Lemons Reynolds, b. 1830, d. 1909. Issue by first marriage:

1. Thomas B Southworth, b. 1837 in MO, d. 1917

2. George R Southworth, b. Jun 1839 in MO, d. 1915

3. Amanda Southworth, b. 1842

4. Elizabeth Jane Southworth, b. 7 Mar 1844 in MO, d. 1928

5. Andrew Jackson Southworth, b. May 1846 in MO, d. 1903

Issue by second marriage:

1. Varness Bay Southworth, b. 1851 in Franklin Co, MO, d. 1864 in OR

2. Martha Pioneer Southworth, b. 18 Apr 1853 in On Plains, OR, d. 1927

3. Swepton Southworth, b. 1859 in OR, d. 1861 in OR

4. Sophronia Washington Southworth, b. 21 Sep 1860 in Lane Co, OR, d. 1945

5. Preston Brooks Southworth, b. 5 Mar 1862 in Josephine Co, OR, d. 1914

6. Mary (Molly) Bridgett Southworth, b. 1864, d. 1872

Page 265 Correction	J. Achilles Southworth should read "John Achilles Southworth"; Catherine Seal should read "Catherine Mahala Seal".

<table>
<tr><td>Correction</td><td>John Achilles Southworth, b. 1807 in Caroline Co, VA, d. 8 Jun 1874 in Caroline Co, VA; m. 22 Dec 1830 in Caroline Co, VA, to Catherine Mahala Seal , b. 1814, d. 1872.

NOTE: For additional information on this family, see the book "As I Find It", starting on page 265.</td></tr>
<tr><td>Page 269</td><td>Leether Loving Southworth (Southard), d. 25 Dec 2005; buried in Westhampton Memorial Park, Richmond, VA</td></tr>
<tr><td>Page 271</td><td>Anne Jackson Morledge, d. 24 Feb 2015</td></tr>
<tr><td>Page 271</td><td>George Alan Morledge, d. 14 Mar 2016</td></tr>
<tr><td>Page 271</td><td>Gustavus Vasa Jackson Jr, d. 26 Jul 2005; buried in St. Paul's Episcopal Church Cemetery, Millers Tavern, VA</td></tr>
<tr><td>Page 271</td><td>Anne Shannon Jackson, d. 11 Jan 2006; buried in Waynesboro, VA</td></tr>
<tr><td>Page 271</td><td>Linda Elizabeth Jackson, m. 8 May 1999 to Wendall Steele Wilson. Their issue:

Elva Anne Wilson, b. 2 Jul 2004 in Richmond, VA</td></tr>
<tr><td>Page 272
Correction</td><td>David Ryan Jackson's birth date should read "3 May 1997"</td></tr>
</table>

Page 273   Alvin William Bass Jr, d. 21 Dec 2010; buried Forest Lawn Cemetery, Richmond, VA

Page 273   Robert Hitter Shackelford Jr, d. 7 Jul 2007; buried Upper King and Queen Baptist Church Cemetery, Helmet, VA

Page 273   Christie Lynn Shackelford, m. 26 Mar 2005 to Alwyn Wynter Davis, Jr. in King and Queen County, VA

Page 274   Edward Bates Southworth (Southard), d. 25 Oct 2010

Page 275   Lucy A Pavy, daughter of Margaret Southworth Pavy and Thomas Lewis Pavy, b. 1854, d. 1932

Page 275   Hester Ann Southworth Sirles, d. 21 May 1912. James Monroe Sirles,
Correction   b. 29 Dec 1835, d. 20 Apr 1903. They are buried in Oakwood Cemetery, Richmond, VA. Their issue:

1. Caroline (Carrie) Belle Sirles
2. Isabella Sirles, b. c. 1858
3. Charles Newton Sirles, b. c. 1859
4. Gertrude Virginia Sirles
5. Sallie B Sirles
6. Ella C Sirles

Caroline (Carrie) Belle Sirles, b. 9 Jan 1858, d. 25 Mar 1896; married a Kane. She is buried in Shockoe Hill Cemetery, Richmond, VA.

Gertrude Virginia Sirles, b. 14 Nov 1860, d. 4 May 1929; m. Fredrick Conrad Germelman, b. 16 Feb 1858, d. 11 Nov 1908. They are buried in Oakwood Cemetery, Richmond, VA.

Sallie B Sirles, b. 27 May 1863, d. 5 Mar 1937; m. Charles Augustus Felvey, b. 21 Feb 1854, d. 25 Jan 1945. They are buried in Riverview Cemetery.

Ella C Sirles, b. 1867, d. 9 Jan 1892; m. 6 Feb 1889 to Eugene Engelking. They are buried in Shockoe Hill Cemetery, Richmond, VA.

Page 276   Esther Southworth, b. 1838, d. ___________

Page 282   Stafford H Garnett Jr, d. 1967

Page 283   Betty Lee Haynes Taylor, d. 14 Aug 2018

Page 283   J Taylor should read "Jackie Taylor Mitchell"
Correction

Page 284   Virginia Dale Taylor, m. 4 Aug 1960 to William Arthur Claytor in Alexandria, VA. William Arthur Claytor, d. 24 Nov 2002 in Colonial Heights, VA

Page 284   William Arthur Claytor Jr, d. 2007

Page 284   Curtis Roger Taylor Sr, d. 10 Dec 2004; buried in Mt Hermon
                Baptist Church Cemetery, Shumansville, VA

Page 285   Linda Jane Taylor Martin, b. 19 Jul 1946

Page 286   Nancy Jean Martin, b. 2 Mar 1940, d. 5 Jan 2018; buried in Mt
                Hermon Baptist Church Cemetery, Shumansville, VA

Page 286   Ann Seal Martin, d. 2 Nov 2014; buried in Mt Hermon Baptist
                Church Cemetery, Shumansville, VA

Page 286   Tony Scott Martin, d. 22 Dec 2015; buried in Mt Hermon Baptist
                Church Cemetery, Shumansville, VA.

Page 286   Issue of Tony Scott Martin & Tammy Cutler Martin:

                Cole Martin, b. 8 Apr 1999

Page 287   Margaret Garnett Martin Smith, d. 28 Aug 2004; buried in Mt
                Hermon Baptist Church Cemetery, Shumansville, VA

Page 288   Marvin Warren Pitts Jr, d. 13 Nov 2014; buried in Mt Hermon
                Baptist Church Cemetery, Shumansville, VA

Page 288   Carolyn Faye Pitts Thomas, d. 28 Aug 2013

Page 289   Joyce Garnett Clark, d. 21 Jun 2011; buried in Mt Hermon Baptist
                    Church Cemetery, Shumansville, VA

Page 289   Issue of Welford D. Taylor & Anna Bell Pierce Taylor:

                    1.   Welford Daring Taylor Jr
                    2.   Gordon R Taylor

Page 289   Welford Daring Taylor Jr, b. 1952; d. 25 Dec 2015; m. ___________.
                    Their issue:

                    1.   Matthew C Taylor
                    2.   Crystal M Taylor

Page 289   Stewart Trevillian Chamberlain's birth date should read "8 Aug 1917"
Correction

Page 290   Hugh Walker Taylor Sr, d. 5 Mar 2010; buried Forest Lawn Cemetery,
                    Richmond, VA

Page 290   Hugh Walker Taylor Jr, d. ___________

Page 290   Taylor M Hague, d. ___________

Page 290   Virginia Taylor Hobson Johnson, d. 17 Jun 2011; buried in Washington
                  Memorial Park, Richmond, VA

Page 291   Thomas Raynard Hobson Jr, d. 3 Nov 2010; buried in Washington
                  Memorial Park, Richmond, VA

Page 291   Issue of Susan Lynn Hobson Repak and Paul Alexander Repak:
                  Sydney Repak, b, ____________

Page 291   Issue of Sarah Lynn Hobson Dickens and Jeffrey Wyatt Dickens:
                  Wyatt Dickens, b. ____________

Page 291   Andrew Christian Taylor Jr, d. 30 Nov 2007; buried in Forest Lawn
                  Cemetery, Richmond, VA

Page 295   Aubrey Bernard Southworth, b. 23 Nov 1918, d. 2 Dec 1984 in TX;
                  m. 28 Dec 1938 in Pittsylvania Co, VA, to May Walker, b. c .1920

Page 295   Charles Boyd Mitchell Sr, d. 14 Oct 2006

Page 295   Catherine Barlow Mitchell, d. 2 Feb 2015; buried in Signal Hill
                  Memorial Park, Hanover, VA

Page 296   Doris Southworth Wilcox, d. 20 Aug 2016; buried in FL

Page 296   Irene Southworth Young, d. 18 May 2005

Page 300   Cinderella Southworth should read "Lucinda Cinderella Southworth"

Page 302   Gertrude Pitts Thomas, d. 16 Aug 2016; buried in Peninsula Memorial
                Park, Newport News, VA

Page 303   Adam Thomas Carnegie, m. 29 Nov 2008 to Karen (Kacey) Robbins.
                Their issue:

                Ellison Carol Carnegie, b. 4 Mar 2014 in Norfolk, VA

Page 303   Alice Carroll Carnegie, m. David Paul Harris. Their issue:

                1.   Easton Taylor Harris, b. 28 Mar 2013 in Suffolk, VA
                2.   Blake Lambert Harris, b. 29 Aug 2017 in Suffolk, VA

Page 303   Aaron William Carnegie, m. Sandra Collick. Their issue:

                Bryce William Carnegie, b. 20 Oct 2012 in Suffolk, VA

Page 303   Carroll Lawrence (Billy) Pitts, d. 29 May 2010; buried in Mt Hermon
                Baptist Church Cemetery, Shumansville, VA

Page 304   The picture shown on Page 304 is not Cinderella Southworth Pitts.
                This has been corrected and the picture included in this update
                is the correct picture for Lucinda Cinderella Southworth Pitts.

Page 305   Lelia Floyd Pitts Loving, d. 19 Sep 2008; buried in Mt Hermon
                Baptist Church Cemetery, Shumansville, VA

Page 306   Jeanne Pitts Tolley, d. 1 Jul 2011; buried in Westhampton Memorial
                Park, Richmond, VA

Page 306   Thomas Leonard Tolley, d. 25 Oct 2006; buried in Westhampton
                Memorial Park, Richmond, VA

Page 306   Ian Thomas Armstrong, b. 13 Aug 2009; son of Laura Hoke

Page 306   William Maynard Carter Sr, d. 12 Aug 2011; buried in Greenlawn
                Cemetery, Bowling Green, VA

Page 307   Cooper Franklyn Townsend, b. 16 Aug 2006; son of Courtney Andrews
                Townsend and Christopher Townsend

Page 307   Kenneth Stephen Stewart, Jr, m. 1 Nov 2004 to Susan Elizabeth Guess,
                b. 4 Apr 1976. Their issue:

                1.   Kaylie Elizabeth Stewart, b. 7 Mar 2004
                2.   Madison Ann Stewart, b. 2 Dec 2008

Page 307   Joseph Wade Burton's birth date should read " 13 Jun 1973"
Correction

Page 307   Issue of Jamie Wray Farmer Burton and Joseph Wade Burton:

1.   Josie Wray Burton, b. 30 Sep 2007
2.   Cayden James Burton, b. 3 Jun 2010)   Twins
3.   Carter Joseph Burton, b. 3 Jun 2010)

Page 307   Meredith Ryan Lane Carter's birthdate should read "25" Apr "1977".

Page 307   Issue of William Maynard Carter III and Meredith Ryan Lane Carter:

1.   William Maynard Carter, IV, b. 23 Feb 2005
2.   Harrison Lane Carter, b. 3 May 2007
3.   Graham Patrick Carter, b. 16 Sep 2011
4.   Mary Katherine Spencer Carter, b. 1 Mar 2017

Lucinda Cinderella Southworth Pitts

Page 307   Jennifer Meade Carter, m. (2) 13 May 2008 to Chip Hartle. Issue by
                  second marriage:

                  1.   Ella Grace Hartle, b. 14 May 2009
                  2.   Kaelynn Hope Hartle, b. 26 Mar 2012

Page 307   Scott Tyler Pitts married Jennifer ___________. Their issue:

                  Kieran Ryan Pitts, b. 16 Mar 2010

Page 309   Ryan Lee Bowie, d. 2 Jan 2005; buried Hulls Memorial Baptist Church
                  Cemetery in Falmouth, VA

Page 309   Mary Gatewood Pitts, d. 27 Feb 2009

Page 309   Ann Pitts Hagerty, d. 13 Mar 2015; buried in PA

Page 309   Charles Lewis Hagerty, d. 25 May 2008; buried in PA

Page 310   Donald James Pitts, d. 25 Dec 2015; buried in Salem Baptist Church
                  Cemetery, Sparta, VA

Page 310   Gary Hugh Watts, b. 27 Apr 1959

Page 310   Joshua Dwayne Watts, m. 28 Jun 2000 to Brandy Michelle Perry, b.

9 Feb 1979. Their issue:

1. Courtney Grace Watts, b. 9 Aug 2007) Twins
2. Charles Tucker Watts, b. 9 Aug 2007)

Page 310   Jared Hugh Watts, m. 8 Dec 2007 to Whitney Sterling Schoonover, b. 28 Jan 1985. Their issue:

1,   Kennedy Sterling Watts, b. 26 Mar 2013
2.   Reese Aileen Watts, b. 13 Jan 2016
3.   Walker Hugh Watts, b. 29 Aug 2018

Page 311   Burle Daniel (Danny) Trivette's birthdate should read "7" Nov "1962".
Correction

Page 311   Issue of Dawn Pitts Trivette and Burle Daniel (Danny) Trivette:

1.   James Austin Trivette, b. 9 Oct 1991
2.   Jason Daniel Trivette, b. 17 Jan 1994
3.   Jacob Robert Trivette, b. 4 Dec 1995

Page 311   Dawn Pitts Trivette, m. (2) 25 May 2011 to Roy A Haun, b. 11 Dec 1971

Page 311   James Austin Trivette, d. 9 Apr 2013; buried in Salem Baptist Church Cemetery, Sparta, VA

Page 311   Jennifer Leigh Pitts, d. 18 Jun 2008

Page 314   Wilbert Lloyd Whittaker Jr, m. (2) 20 May 2009 to Mary Lee Young
                  Pitts, b. 29 Feb 1952

Page 314   Wilma Delores Whittaker, m. (1) 1 Aug 1975 to Winston Ernest Haynes,
                  b. 2 Mar 1951, d. 26 Jul 1984. Winston is buried in County Line Baptist
                  Church Cemetery, Ruther Glen, VA; m. (2) 6 Jun 1987 to David
                  Leonard Smith, b. 6 Jan 1960, d. 4 Mar 2002. David is buried in County
                  Line Baptist Church Cemetery, Ruther Glen, VA. Issue from second
                  marriage:

                  Kendra Faith Smith

Page 314   Anthony Mark Whittaker, d. 13 May 2005; buried in Mt Vernon
                  Methodist Church Cemetery, Ruther Glen, VA

Page 314   Issue of Dennis Wayne Whittaker and Amy Barlow Whittaker:

                  Seth Ryan Whittaker, b. 12 Sep 1994 (Adopted 26 Aug 2008)

Page 315   Marcia Pitts Englert, d. 21 Mar 2018; buried in Greenwood Memorial
                  Gardens, Goochland Co, VA

Page 316   Issue of Ardis and James Fishburne:

                  1.   Catherine Christine Fishburne, b. 12 Jul 2000
                  2.   James Gahan Fishburne III, b. 18 Sep 2002 in Richmond, VA
                  3.   Robert Douglas Fishburne, b. 20 Jul 2007 in Richmond VA

Page 316   John Jason Burford, b. 24 Oct 1975 in Richmond, VA; m. 17 Apr 2004
                  to Amy Suzanne Harrell, b. 2 Aug 1976. Their issue:

                  1. John Thomas Burford, b. 24 Feb 2009 in Richmond, VA
                  2. Caroline Batson Burford, b. 15 Apr, 2011 in Richmond, VA

Page 316   Jocelyn Hilton Pitts, m. 10 Oct 2010 to Gary John Lowzik, Jr, b. 10
                  Feb 1979. Their issue:

                  Emily Alexis Lowzik, b. 4 Nov 2018 in Richmond, VA

Page 316   Mary Beth Pitts Taormina, m. (3) 7 May 2017 to Lawson John Heggie,
                  b. 10 Feb 1954. Mariano (Gus) Taormina d. 22 Sep 2013

Page 316   Tina Marie Embrey Pitts, d. 7 Feb 2017

Page 316   Jeremy Scott Pitts, m. (1) 29 Sep 2007 to Laura Angeline Marsh; m.
                  (2) 3 Dec 2015 to Brandy Nicole Wade, b. 12 Oct 1976. Issue by
                  second marriage:

                  Ashton Wade Pitts, b. 22 Feb 2014

Page 316   Issue of Ronald Scott Pitts and Laurie Dillard Pitts:

                  Trenton Forrester Pitts, b. 16 Dec 2004 in Richmond, VA

Page 316   Bernard Randolph Pitts, d. 22 Dec 2009; buried in Salem Baptist

Church Cemetery, Sparta, VA

Page 317   Arthur Herman Witmeyer, d. 13 Jun 2013; buried in Quantico National Cemetery

Page 317   Sarah Almeda Pitts, m. 11 Aug 2007 to Ryan Colvin. Their issue:

1. Randolph Barrett (Rett) Colvin, b. 31 Jul 2011
2. Ryland Bruce (Riley) Colvin, b. 25 Aug 2013
3. Caroline Elizabeth Colvin, b. 26 Aug 2016
4. Robert Burton (Robbie) Colvin, b. 5 Apr 2018

Page 317   Anne Elizabeth Pitts, m. 9 Sep 2006 to Jacob Landon Grove. Their issue:

1. Charlotte Anne Grove, b. 16 Apr 2012
2. Jack Randolph Grove, b. 10 Oct 2014

Page 317   Jennifer Carol Pitts, m. 22 Oct 2016 to Matthew Scott Anns, b. 16 Apr 1987. Her issue:

Adam James Pitts, b. 31 Jan 2006

Their issue:

Lily Grace Anns, b. 23 Apr 2018

Page 317   Christopher Nelson Pitts, m. 2 May 2015 to Laura Owens, b. 24 Oct 1988. Their issue:

1. Levi Owen Pitts, b. 10 Jan 2017

2. Caleb Nelson Pitts, b. 27 Sep 2018

Page 318   David Sterling Ganoe Jr, d. 17 Nov 2006; buried in Salem Baptist Church Cemetery, Sparta, VA

Page 318   Matthew David Ganoe, m. 13 Apr 2013 to Mallory Scott Satterwhite, b. 9 Sep 1988

Page 318   Melissa Jaclyn Ganoe, m. 22 Jul 2017 to Tucker Wayne Brown

Page 320   Joyce Pitts Wilson, d. 16 Apr 2018; buried in County Line Baptist Church Cemetery, Ruther Glen, VA

Page 320   Robin Elizabeth Wilson , d. 19 May 1970. She was moved from Central Baptist Church Cemetery, Richmond, VA, to County Line Baptist Church Cemetery, Ruther Glen, VA.

Page 321   Marion Joyce Kelley Baughan, d. 17 Dec 2014; buried in St. Stephen's Baptist Church Cemetery, St. Stephen's Church, VA

Page 321   Kelly Sue Baughan should read "Kelley"
Correction

| Page 322 | Issue of Cara Leigh Dunnavant Alexander and Justin Eugene Alexander: |
| | |

Ainsley Elizabeth Alexander, b. 22 Jun 2004 in Richmond, VA

| Page 322 | Neale Wayne Kelley's birth date should read 10 May "1949". Neale |
| Correction | Wayne Kelley, d. 25 Jun 2017; cremated |

| Page 322 | Jacquelin Pleasants Kelley, d. 8 Nov 2014 |

| Page 323 | Stephanie Ryan Covington, m. (1) 23 Oct 2005 to Daniel Alan Melson, b. 10 Jun 1980; m. (2) 4 Apr 2015 to Benjamin Jeffrey-Preece Sadler, b. 2 Nov 1987 |

| Page 323 | Karla Renee Covington, m. 12 May 2018 to Ryan Perry Eutsler, b. 30 Jul 1985 |

| Page 323 | Courtney Liane Covington, m. 27 Oct 2012 to James Jeremy Taylor, b. 2 Dec 1982. Their issue: |

Sophia Mae Taylor, b. 14 Jul 2019

| Page 323 | Andrew Michael Gill, m. 15 Oct 2005 to Christy Michelle Warren. Their issue: |

1. Taylor Lee-Ann Gill, b. 6 Aug 2003
2. Peyton Sue Gill, b. 17 May 2008

Page 324   Krista Lynn Gill should read "Krysta Lynn Gill"

Page 324   Issue of Krysta Lynn Gill and Jonathan Art Jackson:

                Jocelyn Avery Jackson, b. 15 Dec 2013 in Raleigh, NC

Page 324   Issue of Meagan Renee Gill and Ashley Kyle Beamon:

                Bryce Mason Beamon, b. 18 Sep 2014 in Raleigh, NC

Page 324   Robert Carroll Beazley III, m. 18 Oct 2008 to Valerie Basoco.
                Their issue:

                1.   Robert Carroll Beazley, IV, b. 3 Jan 2009 in CA
                2.   Summer Valentina Beazley, b. 19 Aug 2010 in CA

Page 324   Mark Alan Beazley, m. 9 May 2009 to Amber Nicole Link. Their issue:

                Delaney Lynn Beazley, b. 1 Mar 2010 in Newport News, VA

Page 324   Issue of Johanna Elizabeth Beazley:

                Bailey Elizabeth Tilley, b. 29 Jul 2009

Page 325   Lillian Pitts Pugh Pavy, d. 29 Nov 2016; buried in Mt Hermon Baptist
                Church Cemetery, Shumansville, VA

| Page 325 | Robert Woodford (Dick) Pitts, d. 29 May 2018; buried in Mt Hermon Baptist Church Cemetery, Shumansville, VA |

| Page 326 | Issue of Taylor Madeline Roberts: |

Karson Deaton, b. 26 Dec 2013

| Page 326 | Issue of Christopher Lanny Fulford & Crystal Wilder Fulford: |

Chase Wyatt Fulford, b. 17 Jun 2007

| Page 326 | Katherine Louise Phillips, m. 20 Jun 2015 to Chad Devine, b. ___________. |

Issue of Katherine (Katie) Phillips Devine and Bryan Marzo:

Everly Katherine Marzo, b. 8 Feb 2019

| Page 326 | Nellie Rose (Dolly) Pitts Hartman, d. 5 Oct 1974 |

| Page 326 Correction | James Joseph Hartman should read "Joseph James Hartman" |

| Page 326 | Joseph James Hartman, d. 15 Dec 2006; buried in Holy Cross Cemetery, Cleveland, OH |

| Page 327 | Ian James McHugh, m. (1) 19 Aug 2008 to Tami H Brown; m. (2) 20 |

Jul 2018 to Betsy Woods Lenahan, b. 25 May 1979. Issue from first marriage:

Neala Dolly McHugh, b. 8 Dec 2014 in CA

Page 327   Nellie Ann McHugh, m. 15 Jul 2017 to Tyler Wade Tingley, b. 30 Sep 1977. Their issue:

Owen Ronald Tingley, b. 17 May 2018

Page 327   John David Hartman, m. (2) 12 Oct 2002 to Michelle Louise Hornbach, b. 4 Mar 1971. Issue by second marriage:

1. John Carter Hartman, b. 31 Jul 2006 in Chicago, IL
2. Henry Joseph Hartman, b. 22 Oct 2009 in Chicago, IL

Page 327   Edward Dawson Pitts, d. 26 Nov 2011; cremated

Page 327   Mabel Pitts Weymouth, d. 1 Oct 2018; buried in Mt Hermon Baptist Church Cemetery, Shumansville, VA

Page 328   Julian Roy (Big Boy) Carter Sr, d. 13 Dec 2018; buried in Greenlawn Cemetery, Bowling Green, VA

Page 328   Lisa Kay Carter Burch, m. (2) 21 Nov 2009 to John Woodroof. Issue by second marriage:

Julianne Isabella Woodroof, b. 1 Feb 2011

Page 328   Benny Sale Brooks, d. 1 Sep 2016; cremated

Page 328   Jonathan Benjamin Brooks, m. 4 Jun 2016 to Lauren Elizabeth
                  Didlake, b. 23 Sep 1991. Their issue:

                  Carter Elizabeth Brooks, b. 9 May 2017, Richmond, VA

Page 329   John Eric Oakes, m. 21 Jun 2003 to Kellie Gardner, b. 18 Feb 1977.
                  Their issue:

                  1.   Everett Liam Gardner Oakes, b. 15 Mar 2013
                  2.   Fianna Elsie Andalyn Oakes, b. 12 Nov 2015

Page 329   Michael Brandon Oakes, m. 31 Oct 2008 to Rachel Feero, b. 24 Mar
                  1981. Their issue:

                  1.   Oscar Malcolm Eastwood Oakes, b. 19 Feb 2008
                  2.   Emerson Enzo Feero Oakes, b. 8 Apr 2010
                  3.   Tesla River Violet Oakes, b. 9 Apr 2015

Page 329   Katie Lea Oakes, m. 26 Jul 2008 to Conor McMahon. Their issue:

                  1.   Virginia June Oakes McMahon, b. 14 Oct 2009 in NM
                  2.   Cassius Owen Oakes McMahon, b. 29 Jan 2012 in KY

Page 329   Issue of Scott Andrew Oakes and Dora Bowden Oakes:

                  1.   Kolee Mae Oakes, b. 13 Nov 2002
                  2.   Brandon Zane Oakes, b. 18 Nov 2006

                  Issue of Scott Andrew Oakes and Shannon Marie Alexander:

                  Landon Roger Alexander, b. 2 Jul 2009

Issue of Scott Andrew Oakes and Twanic Poliquin:

Alexiyah Poliquin, b. 24 Aug 2011 in ME

Page 329   Rebecca Lynn Oakes, m. 5 Nov 2011 to Timothy Dean DeWitt, b. 9 Jun 1981. Their issue:

1. Hannah Lea Oakes, b. 29 Jul 2006
2. Norah Elizabeth Oakes, b. 7 Oct 2010
3. Carter Dean DeWitt, b. 30 Apr 2012

Page 329   Sarah Elizabeth Edwards, m. 25 May 2013 to Stephen Michael Salvato. Their issue:

1. Lillian Elizabeth Salvato, b. 3 Jul 2014 in Richmond, VA
2. Eleanor Catherine Salvato, b. 6 Mar 2019 in Richmond, VA

Page 329   Issue of Charles Russell Dalton and Jennifer Nicole Champion, b. 16 Apr 1985

Brandon Scott Champion-Dalton, b. 7 May 2004 in Richmond, VA

Page 329   Issue of Charles Russell Dalton and Holly Coleman:

Annabelle Hope Dalton, b. 9 Jan 2017

Page 329   Melanie Laverne Pitts Church m. (2) 11 Aug 2007 to Eric Allen Wilson

Page 330   Kristina Marie Church, m. 14 Nov 2015 to Christopher Wyatt Robens,

b. 31 Aug 1989. Their issue:

1. Nolen Weston Robens, b. 26 Jul 2013
2. Ethan Colton Robens, b. 8 Nov 2016

Page 330   Dawn Aniello Pitts, d. 25 Dec 2017; cremated

Page 330   Thomas Lee Pitts III, m. Jessica Mondajar. Their issue:

1. Addison Jean Pitts, b. 3 Feb 2017 in Richmond, VA
2. Raylyne Marie Pitts, b. 23 Oct 2018 in Richmond, VA

Page 334   Carl Stansbury Pates Jr birth date should read "21 Aug 1944"
Correction

Page 336   Lillian Street Southworth, d. 29 Dec 2004; buried in Lakewood
Cemetery, Bowling Green, VA

Page 338   Angela Kay Southworth, m. 22 Jun 2002 to Jason Ryan Houston, b.
30 Jun 1976

Page 338   Issue of Tammie Southworth Loe and Ronald Jason Loe:

Robert Jesse Loe, b. ___________

Page 338   Ronald Jason Loe, d. 26 Dec 2018

Page 338   Willard Jasper Farmer, d. 15 May 2009; buried in Greenlawn

Cemetery, Bowling Green, VA

<table>
<tr><td>Page 339</td><td>Ray Carlton Southworth, d. 28 Jan 2007 in Fredericksburg, VA; buried in Sunset Memorial Gardens, Fredericksburg, VA</td></tr>
<tr><td>Page 340
Correction</td><td>Kimberly Robyn Speaks birth date should read "9 Aug 1974"</td></tr>
<tr><td>Page 342</td><td>Clayton Wayne Beazley, d. 8 Oct 2017; buried in Salem Baptist Church Cemetery, Sparta, VA</td></tr>
<tr><td>Page 344</td><td>James W Southworth, b. 1906</td></tr>
</table>

Tombstones of J A Southworth & Catharine Seal Southworth

Richmond Va

decmBer 26 1903

My dear Brother ira i recived letter and was more than glad to hear from you and your famly i would like so much to see you all you say you has one child a son i hope he is a good young man and will take after his unfle becor he was good you say o ald and feble you ar not much oalder than i am i was seventy the ninth day of last month novemBer hester was sixty eigt the ninth of this desember she is a goot eal Better than she haspin for som time lucy and her famly ar all rite well she has fore marid chrildren three girls and one son all doing verry well i hav seven gran chrildren and ten great gran chrildern and onley one child lucy

Page One of Letter from Margaret Reid dated December 26, 1903

your son comes to richmond some time
he mite call to se us we would Be
very glead to se him this is my
seventh chrismas and i in gay self
very well and i hope you and all
the res of of famley has don the same
you must write to me a gain i was
at cinday and i would has com to
se you But did not feal so well and
went Back home i got a letter from
linda som time a go and she said
you did not feal so well But i hope
you ar fealing Better now and we
will
se each other a gain By and By
When the wether gets fine i do not
se gnley franklin oftin she all ways
Bisy she has no tim to chat and
i chat a good eal look over Bad
wrigting for i use no specks write
to me a gaine my nomBers 520
Church street gabe my love to all
            Margaret Reid

Page Two of letter from Margaret Reid dated December 26, 1903

Richmond Va

desember 29th 1903

i must rite you a line to tell
you i send you my picture
i did not have it at the time
the first the 2 one of my
daughters had it so i will
me to day so i will [ma] to
marow the 30 you let me no if you
get it that was taken 8 years
a go and tell me if you think it
looks lik me i would be glad to
se you and your famly tell your son
to call to se us when he comes to
Richmond we will be glad to
se him well i hav to say good
By for this time you mus rite
to me i hope you ar fealing
Better   love to all we ar all
rite well to day hope you all ar the
same Margaret Reid 620
Church St

Ltter from Margaret Reid dated December 29th, 1903

VIRGINIA,

CAROLINE COUNTY—To wit:

TO ANY PERSON AUTHORIZED TO CELEBRATE MARRIAGES:

You are hereby authorized *to join together, in the Holy State of Matrimony, according to the rites and ceremonies of your Church or religious denomination, and the laws of this Commonwealth,* Ira Southworth and Mahala Cecil

Given under my hand, as Clerk of the County Court of said County, this 8th day of January 1867.

Robt Hudgin CLERK.
by R T Hudgin D C

Date of proposed marriage,   10th January 1867
Place of proposed marriage,   Caroline County
Age of man,   36 Years
Place of his birth,   Caroline   ; and condition,   Single
Place of his residence,   ; and occupation,   Blacksmith
Names of his parents,   Achilles Southworth Caroline County & Catharine Southworth
Age of woman,   22 Years   ; and condition,   Single
Place of her birth,   Caroline County   and residence,   Caroline County
Names of her parents,   Jas. Cecil and Patsy Cecil

Teste,   Robt Hudgin
by R T Hudgin D C   CLERK.

I   Ro. H Bonce   a Minister of the   Baptist Church Church, hereby certify, That on the 10 day of Jany 1867, and in pursuance of the annexed License, I solemnized a Marriage between the above-described parties Ira Southworth and Mahala Cecil

Given under my hand, this 10 day of Jany 1867

Ro. H Bonce

[To be returned to the Clerk within ten days after celebrating the Marriage.]

Marriage License of Ira Southworth & Mahala Cecil

MARRIAGE LICENSE.

VIRGINIA, *Caroline County* to wit:

To any Person Licensed to Celebrate Marriages:

You are hereby authorized to join together in the Holy State of Matrimony, according to the rites and ceremonies of your Church, or religious denomination, and the laws of the Commonwealth of Virginia, *George Dillard* and *Suberna Southworth*

Given under my hand, as Clerk of the *County* Court of *Caroline* this *26th* day of *Dec.* 18*70*

Robt. Hudgin CLERK.

CERTIFICATE TO OBTAIN A MARRIAGE LICENSE,

To be annexed to the License, required by Act passed 15th March, 1861.

Time of Marriage, *about*

Place of Marriage, *neat Oakley, Caroline County*

Full names of Parties Married *Labove*

Age of Husband, *twenty three years*

Age of Wife *twenty three years*

Condition of Husband (widowed or single), *Single*

Condition of Wife, (widowed or single), *do*

Place of Husband's Birth, *Caroline County*

Place of Wife's Birth, *Caroline County*

Place of Husband's Residence, *Do*

Place of Wife's Residence, *do*

Names of Husband's Parents, *Edmund & Virginia Dillard*

Names of Wife's Parents, *Achilles & Catharine Southworth*

Occupation of Husband, *Farmer*

Given under my hand, this *26* day of *Dec.*, 18*70*

Robt. Hudgin CLERK.

MINISTER'S RETURN OF MARRIAGE.

I CERTIFY, that on the *29* day of *December*, 18*71*, at *Achilles Southworth, Nenalie*, I united in Marriage the above named and described parties, under authority of the annexed License. *A. Broaddus Bap. Minister*

2 months

☞ The Minister celebrating a Marriage is required, within ten days thereafter, to return the License to the Office of the Clerk who issued the same with an endorsement thereon of the FACT of such marriage, and of the TIME and PLACE of celebrating the same.

Marriage License of George Dillard & Sabernie Southworth

MARRIAGE LICENSE.

'ginia, *Caroline County* ______ to wit:

TO ANY PERSON LICENSED TO CELEBRATE MARRIAGES:

You are hereby authorized to join together in the Holy State of Matrimony, accordin[g]
rites and ceremonies of your Church, or religious denomination, and the laws of the Comm[on]
lth of Virginia *Stafford H. Garnett*

Julia F. Southworth

Given under my hand, as Clerk of the _____ *County* ______ C[o]

Caroline this *27th* day of *June* 18*72*

Robt. Hodgin ______ Clerk

CERTIFICATE TO OBTAIN A MARRIAGE LICENSE,

To be annexed to the License, required by Act passed 15th March, 1861.

of Marriage, _____ *About 5 July next.*

of Marriage, _____ *Caroline County*

Marriage License of Stafford H Garnett & Julia F Southworth

6882

CERTIFICATE OF DEATH
COMMONWEALTH OF VIRGINIA
DEPARTMENT OF HEALTH
BUREAU OF VITAL STATISTICS

1 PLACE OF DEATH
COUNTY OF *King William*
MAGISTERIAL DISTRICT OF *Acquinton*

REGISTRATION DISTRICT No. *5015* REGISTERED No. *1*

2 FULL NAME *Callie Southworth*

(A) RESIDENCE. NO. *Aylett Va*

PERSONAL AND STATISTICAL PARTICULARS	MEDICAL CERTIFICATE OF DEATH
3. SEX *Female* 4. COLOR OR RACE *White* 5. *widow*	21. DATE OF DEATH *Mar 8 1933*

7. AGE *60*

8. TRADE, PROFESSION *Housekeeper*

12. BIRTHPLACE *Caroline Co. Va*

13. NAME *Lindsey Pitts*

14. BIRTHPLACE *Unknown*

15. MAIDEN NAME *Mercury Chenault*

16. BIRTHPLACE *unknown*

17. INFORMANT *John Southworth*

18. BURIAL, CREMATION, OR REMOVAL *Vernon Church* DATE *March 9 1933*

19. UNDERTAKER *O. Profit & Sons*

20. FILED *March 8 1933*

Certificate of Death for Callie Southworth.

276-37   1907-1923

INTERMENT CARD
OAKWOOD

Name Reid, Margaret F.

Age 74 Years________ Months________ Days. Date Buried June 18, 1908

Place of death________ 606 S. 1st St.

Cause of death________

Location: Plat________ Range________ Section________ Division C Lot 8

Quarter 3 Single grave portion________ Row________ Grave 8

Section Owner Mrs. E. Redford

Remarks Gr. 3rd. from S. C.

____

____ P. B. No.________

INTERMENT CARD
OAKWOOD

Name Garnett, Julia F.

Age 68 Years________ Months________ Days. Date Buried July 12th 1918.

Place of death________ 2521 O. Street

Cause of death________

Location: Plat ~~B~~ 64 Range________ Section________ Division 43 Lot

Quarter________ Single grave portion ~~6~~ Row 4 Grave ~~S. G.~~

Section Owner R.B. Baldwin.

Remarks Feb 4th, 1924, moved to above.

____

____ P. B. No.________

Interment Cards for Margaret F Reid & Julia F Garnett

Hester Ann Southworth Sirles

- **Description:** Germelman family section
- **Cemetery Name:** Oakwood Cemetery - Richmond, Virginia
- **Name on Headstone:** Hester Ann Sirles
- **Birth Year:** 1835
- **Death Year:** 1912

Tombstone of Hester Ann Southworth Sirles

CERTIFICATE OF DEATH
COMMONWEALTH OF VIRGINIA

2 FULL NAME Evelyn Pitts Southworth

PERSONAL AND STATISTICAL PARTICULARS

8 OCCUPATION OF DECEASED — Housewife

10 NAME OF FATHER Willis Pitts

12 MAIDEN NAME OF MOTHER Susan Wright

MEDICAL CERTIFICATE OF DEATH

Cirrhosis of the liver

CONTRIBUTORY High Blood Pressure

Certificate of death for Evelyn Pitts Southworth

THE TAYLOR FAMILY CORRECTIONS & ADDITIONAL INFORMATION

Page 172   William T Taylor (Farmer), b. 1780, d. c. 1844 in Caroline Co, VA, m. to Nancy Hutcherson, b. 1780, d. 20 Dec 1861 in Caroline Co, VA, of old age: Their known issue:

Thomas Burton Taylor

Thomas Burton Taylor, b. 1795, d. 24 Jan 1854 in Caroline Co, VA; m. 10 Jan 1815 to Margaret (Peggy) Ann Houston

NOTE: For additional information on this family, see the book "As I Find It, Part II".

Page 174   Lelia Taylor, m. 17 May 1896 to William B Pitts

Page 177   Mary Alice Poats Ball, d. 24 Jan 2013; buried in Salem Baptist Church Cemetery, Sparta, VA

Page 177   Thomas Joseph Ball, d. 3 Feb 2013; buried in Salem Baptist Church Cemetery, Sparta, VA

Page 177   James Samuel Ball, d. 17 Aug 2010; buried in Salem Baptist Church
                   Cemetery, Sparta, VA

Page 182   William Webb Beazley, d. 15 Aug 2010; buried in Mt Hermon
                   Baptist Church Cemetery, Shumansville, VA

Page 184   Raymond Luther Beazley, d. 2 Nov 2012; buried in Lakewood
                   Cemetery, Bowling Green, VA

Page 185   Virginia Dale Beazley, m. ____________"Ansley".
Correction

Page 187   Gertrude Pitts Thomas, d. 16 Aug 2016; buried in Peninsula Memorial
                   Park, Newport News, VA

Page 187   Adam Thomas Carnegie, m. 29 Nov 2008 to Karen (Kacey) Robbins.
                   Their issue:

                   Ellison Carol Carnegie, b. 4 Mar 2014 in Norfolk, VA

Page 188   Alice Carroll Carnegie, m. David Paul Harris. Their issue:

                   1.   Easton Taylor Harris, b. 28 Mar 2013 in Suffolk, VA
                   2.   Blake Lambert Harris, b. 29 Aug 2017 in Suffolk, VA

Page 188   Aaron William Carnegie, m. Sandra Collick. Their issue:

                  Bryce William Carnegie, b. 20 Oct 2012 in Suffolk, VA

Page 188   Carroll Lawrence (Billy) Pitts, d. 29 May 2010; buried in Mt Hermon
                  Baptist Church Cemetery, Shumansville, VA

Page 188   Lelia Floyd Pitts Loving, d. 19 Sep 2008; buried in Mt Hermon
                  Baptist Church Cemetery, Shumansville, VA

Page 195   Jane Barlow Madison, d. 16 Aug 2012; buried in Lakewood Cemetery,
                  Bowling Green, VA

Page 195   Keith Edward Madison's birthdate should read 26 "July" 1959.
Correction

Page 196   Jeffrey Allen Taylor, d. 19 Oct 2018

Page 196   Michael Clift Hardin, d. 1 Mar 2009; buried in Trinity United Methodist
                  Church Cemetery, King George, VA

Page 196   Manley Dillard Taylor, d. 4 Oct 2016; buried in Lakewood Cemetery,
                  Bowling Green, VA

Page 196   Lois Covington Taylor, d. 12 Sep 2009; buried in Lakewood Cemetery, Bowling Green, VA

Page 196   Leah Michelle Taylor, m. 11 Oct 2008 to Russell Brian Acors. Their issue:

                  Jordan Acors, b. ___________

Page 196   Kristen Denise Taylor, m. 6 Jun 2009 to Ian Christopher Kraynak

Page 197   Joyce Ann Pitts Wilson, d. 16 Apr 2018; buried in County Line Baptist Church Cemetery, Ruther Glen, VA

Page 198   Robin Elizabeth Wilson, d. 19 May 1970. She was moved from Central Baptist Church Cemetery, Richmond, VA, to County Line Baptist Church Cemetery, Ruther Glen, VA.

Page 198   Marion Joyce Kelley Baughan, d. 17 Dec 2014; buried in St Stephens Baptist Church Cemetery, St Stephens Church, VA

Page 199   Neale Wayne Kelley's birthdate should read 10 May "1949". Neale
Correction   Wayne Kelley, d. 25 Jun 2017; cremated

Page 199   Jacquelin Pleasants Kelley, d. 8 Nov 2014

Page 200   Stephanie Ryan Covington, m. (2) 4 Apr 2015 to Benjamin Jeffrey-Preece Sadler, b. 2 Nov 1987

Page 200   Karla Renee Covington, m. 12 May 2018 to Ryan Perry Eutsler, b.
                  30 Jul 1985

Page 200   Courtney Liane Covington, m. 27 Oct 2012 to James Jeremy Taylor,
                  b. 2 Dec 1982. Their issue:

                  Sophia Mae Taylor, b. 14 Jul 2019

Page 200   Krista Lynn Gill should read "Krysta Lynn Gill"

Page 200   Issue of Krysta Lynn Gill and Jonathan Art Jackson:

                  Jocelyn Avery Jackson, b. 15 Dec 2013 in Raleigh, NC

Page 200   Issue of Meagan Renee Gill and Ashley Kyle Beamon:

                  Bryce Mason Beamon, b. 18 Sep 2014 in Raleigh, NC

Page 200   Andrew Michael Gill, m. 15 Oct 2005 to Christy Michelle Warren.
                  Their issue:

                  1.   Taylor Lee-Ann Gill, b. 6 Aug 2003
                  2.   Peyton Sue Gill, b. 17 May 2008

Page 201   Robert Carroll Beazley, III, m. 18 Oct 2008 to Valerie Basoco.
                  Their issue:

                  1.   Robert Carroll Beazley, IV, b. 3 Jan 2009 in CA
                  2.   Summer Valentina Beazley, b. 19 Aug 2010 in CA

Page 201   Harold Wade Beazley Jr, m. (2) ___________

Page 201   Mark Alan Beazley, m. 9 May 2009 to Amber Nicole Link. Their issue:

                  Delaney Lynn Beazley, b. 1 Mar 2010 in Newport News, VA

Page 201   Issue of Johanna Elizabeth Beazley:

                  Bailey Elizabeth Tilley, b. 29 Jul 2009 in Newport News, VA

Page 201   Lillian Pitts Pugh Pavy, d. 29 Nov 2016; buried in Mt Hermon Baptist
                  Church Cemetery, Shumansville, VA

Page 202   Robert Woodford (Dick) Pitts, d. 29 May 2018; buried in Mt Hermon
                  Baptist Church Cemetery, Shumansville, VA

Page 202   Issue of Taylor Madeline Roberts:

                  Karson Deaton, b. 26 Dec 2013

Page 202   Issue of Christopher Lanny Fulford and Crystal Wilder Fulford:

                  Chase Wyatt Fulford, b. 17 Jun 2007

Page 202   Katherine Louise Phillips, m. 20 Jun 2015 to Chad Devine, b. ___________.

                  Issue of Katherine (Katie) Phillips Devine and Bryan Marzo:

                  Everly Katherine Marzo, b. 8 Feb 2019

Page 203   Joseph James Hartman, d. 15 Dec 2006; buried in Holy Cross Cemetery, Cleveland, OH

Page 203   Ian James McHugh, m. (1) 19 Aug 2008 to Tami H Brown; m. (2) 20 Jul 2018 to Betsy Woods Lenahan, b. 25 May 1979. Issue by first marriage:

Neala Dolly McHugh, b. 8 Dec 2014 in CA

Page 203   Nellie Ann McHugh, m. 15 Jul 2017 to Tyler Wade Tingley, b. 30 Sep 1977. Their issue:

Owen Ronald Tingley, b. 17 May 2018

Page 203   Issue of John David Hartman and Michelle Hornbeck Hartman:

1. John Carter Hartman, b. 31 Jul 2066 in Chicago, IL
2. Henry Joseph Hartman, b. 22 Oct 2009 in Chicago, IL

Page 203   Edward Dawson Pitts, d. 26 Nov 2011; cremated

Page 204   Mabel Pitts Weymouth, d. 1 Oct 2018; buried in Mt Hermon Baptist Church Cemetery, Shumansville, VA

Page 204   Julian Roy (Big Boy) Carter Sr, d. 13 Dec 2018; buried in Greenlawn Cemetery, Bowling Green, VA

Page 204   Lisa Kay Carter Burch, m. (2) 21 Nov 2009 to John Woodroof. Issue from second marriage:

Julianne Isabella Woodroof, b. 1 Feb 2011

Page 204   Benny Sale Brooks, d. 1 Sep 2016; cremated

Page 204   Jonathan Benjamin Brooks, m. 4 Jun 2016 to Lauren Elizabeth Didlake, b. 23 Sep 1991. Their issue:

Carter Elizabeth Brooks, b. 9 May 2017

Page 204   Irene Zicafoose Pitts, d. 2 Feb 2011; buried in Mt Hermon Baptist Church Cemetery, Shumansville, VA

Page 205   Issue of John Eric Oakes and Kellie Gardner Oakes:

1. Everett Liam Gardner Oakes, b. 15 Mar 2013 in ME
2. Fianna Elsie Andalyn Oakes, b. 12 Nov 2015 in ME

Page 205   Michael Brandon Oakes, m. 31 Oct 2008 to Rachel Feero, b. 24 Mar 1981. Their issue:

1. Oscar Malcolm Eastwood Oakes, b. 19 Feb 2008 in ME
2. Emerson Enzo Feero Oakes, b. 8 Apr 2010 in ME
3. Tesla River Violet Oakes, b. 9 Apr 2015 in ME

Page 205   Katie Lea Oakes, m. 26 Jul 2008 to Conor McMahon, b. 15 Aug 1978.
             Their issue:

             1.   Virginia June Oakes McMahon, b. 14 Oct 2009 in NM
             2.   Cassius Owen Oakes McMahon, b. 29 Jan 2012 in KY

Page 205   Issue of Scott Andrew Oakes and Dora Bowden Oakes:

             1.   Kolee Mae Oakes, b. 13 Nov 2002 in Waterville, ME
             2.   Brandon Zane Oakes, b. 18 Nov 2006 in Waterville ME

Page 205   Issue of Scott Andrew Oakes and Shannon Marie Alexander, b. 21
             Sep 1989:

             Landon Roger Alexander, b. 2 Jul 2009 in ME

             Issue of Scott Andrew Oakes and Twanic Poliquin:

             Alexiyah Poliquin, b. 24 Aug 2011 in ME

Page 205   Rebecca Lynn Oakes, m. 5 Nov 2011 to Timothy Dean DeWitt, b.
             9 Jun 1981. Their issue:

             1.   Hannah Lea Oakes, b. 29 Jul 2006 in ME
             2.   Norah Elizabeth Oakes, b. 7 Oct 2010 in ME
             3.   Carter Dean DeWitt, b. 30 Apr 2012 in ME

Page 205   Sarah Elizabeth Edwards, m. 25 May 2013 to Stephen Michael
             Salvato. Their issue:

1. Lillian Elizabeth Salvato, b. 3 Jul 2014 in Richmond, VA
2. Eleanor Catherine Salvato, b. 6 Mar 2019 in Richmond, VA

Page 205   Issue of Charles Russell Dalton and Holly Coleman:

Annabelle Hope Dalton, b. 9 Jan 2017

Page 205   Melanie Laverne Pitts Church, m. (2) 11 Aug 2007 to Eric Allen Wilson

Page 205   Kristina Marie Church, m. 14 Nov 2015 to Christopher Wyatt Robens,
b. 31 Aug 1989. Their issue:

1. Nolen Weston Robens, b. 26 Jul 2013
2. Ethan Colton Robens, b. 8 Nov 2016

Page 206   Dawn Aniello Pitts, d. 25 Dec 2017; cremated

Page 206   Thomas Lee Pitts III, m. Jessica Mondajar. Their issue:

1. Addison Jean Pitts, b. 3 Feb 2017 in Richmond, VA
2. Raylyne Marie Pitts, b. 23 Oct 2018 in Richmond, VA

Page 206   Rae Covington Gatewood, d. 22 Jun 2014; cremated

Page 207   Jeanne Gatewood Clapp, d. 5 Jun 2014; buried in MD

| Page 207 | Roger Carlton Gatewood, d. 16 Jun 2015 in Austin, TX; buried in St Pauline's Cemetery in Windsor, ND |

| Page 207 | Atwell Burruss (Nick) Byrd, m. Carrie Anne McKinney. Their issue: |

1. Kylie MacKenzie Byrd, b. 11 Oct 2008
2. Shane Hunter Byrd, b. 24 Jul 2014

| Page 208 Correction | Elizabeth Ann Wallace should read Elizabeth "Anne" Wallace |

| Page 208 | Elizabeth Taylor Wallace, d. Apr 2015; buried in Arlington National Cemetery |

| Page 208 | Anna Rosalyn Taylor Landram, d. 4 Apr 2009; buried in Greenlawn Cemetery, Bowling Green, VA |

| Page 208 | Vincent Rudolph Miller, d. 10 Dec 2012; buried in NC |

| Page 210 Correction | Jannelle Anne Wallace should read "Junnelle" Anne Wallace |

| Page 210 | Issue of Junnelle Anne Wallace and Edward Cleanan Brooks Jr: |

Edward Cleanan Brooks III, b. 21 Jul 2014

<table>
<tr><td>Page 227</td><td>Wesley Conway Taylor, d. 8 Feb 2008; buried in Taylorsville Baptist Church Cemetery, Doswell, VA</td></tr>
<tr><td>Page 228</td><td>Evelyn Thomas Taylor, d. 5 Apr 2010; buried in MO</td></tr>
<tr><td>Page 231</td><td>William Woodford Taylor, d. 27 Apr 1862</td></tr>
<tr><td>Page 231</td><td>Additional issue born to William Woodford Taylor and Nancy Houston Taylor:

Mary E Taylor, b. 1847, d. 29 Jul 1893; m. 26 Dec 1878 in Caroline Co, VA, by Rev James H Marshall, to Ezer D Anderson, b. 1842, d. ___________. Issue unknown.</td></tr>
<tr><td>Page 232
Correction</td><td>Virginia H Vaughan, b. Nov "1846"</td></tr>
<tr><td>Page 234</td><td>William Gordon Taylor, d. 10 Jun 2008</td></tr>
<tr><td>Page 234</td><td>Stephanie Taylor VanZile, m. 7 May 2011 to Leslie Bryant Stone</td></tr>
<tr><td>Page 242</td><td>David Ray Taylor, Jr., d. 24 Dec 2010; buried in Carmel Baptist Church Cemetery, Ruther Glen, VA</td></tr>
</table>

Page 242   Issue of Jacqueline Taylor Clingenpeel and David Wayne Clingenpeel

Taylor Clingenpeel, b. ____________

Page 242   Taylor Blanton Doggett, m. 27 Oct 2018 to Caitlin Ann McClelland, b. 2 Nov 1991

Page 243   Paul Alan Cox, d. 17 Nov 2014; buried in Mt Vernon Methodist Church Cemetery, Ruther Glen, VA

Page 244   James Jeremy Taylor, m. 27 Oct 2012 to Courtney Liane Covington, b. 7 Jun 1986. Their issue:

Sophia Mae Taylor, b. 14 Jul 2019

Page 245   Kristina Nicole Taylor, m. 4 May 2013 to Gregory Wayne Brooking, b. 2 Jul 1984. Their issue:

Tristan James Brooking, b. 16 Sep 2015

Page 245   Kasie Blair Taylor, m. 23 Jun 2018 to Zachary David Jordan, b. 18 Feb 1991

Page 246   Roger Lee Taylor, d. 24 Apr 2009; buried in Signal Hill Memorial Park, Hanover, VA

Page 248   Otha Booth Vial, Jr, d. 20 Feb 2009 (Cancer); buried in Westhampton Memorial Park, Richmond, VA. Their issue:

1. Gregory Lynn Vial, d. ___________
2. Glenda Vial (Shaw)
3. Joanne Vial (Paulette)
4. Rick Vial

Page 248   Elizabeth Maria Taylor, d. 25 Nov 2016; buried in Signal Hill Memorial Park, Hanover, VA

Page 248   Woodford David Taylor Jr, d. 1 Apr 2017; buried in Signal Hill Memorial Park, Hanover, VA

Page 248   Melinda Taylor, m. James Armitage

Page 248   Brenda Ann Taylor, b. 1963; d. 2 May 2009; buried in Signal Hill Memorial Park, Hanover, VA

Page 249   Hilda Corker Taylor, d. 23 Oct 2013

Page 249   Thomas Taylor should read "Thomas Edward Taylor"
Correction

Page 249   Jackson Taylor should read "Thomas Jackson Taylor"
Correction

Page 249   Julie Anna Martin Taylor, d. ____________

Page 250   Juanita Kulp Taylor, d. 22 Oct 2008

Page 251   Robert Edward Young, d. 24 Apr 2007

Page 251   Clifton Carper Taylor, d. 21 Feb 2009; buried in Signal Hill Memorial
                  Park, Hanover, VA

Page 252   Dillard Vaughan Taylor should read "Dylan"
Correction

Page 254   Dorothy Silva Taylor, d. 16 Dec 2010

Page 254   Robert Watts Jacovers should read "Jacobus"
Corrections   Rhonda Lee Jacovers should read "Jacobus"
                  Raina Leigh Jacovers should read "Jacobus"
                  Robert Watts Jocovers Jr should read "Jacobus"

Page 256   Alberta Gertrude Loving, d. 29 Jul 2010; buried in Signal Hill Memorial
                  Park, Hanover, VA

Page 257   Willis Pearl Loving Williams Chenault, d. ____________

Mildred M Taylor, b. 1820 in Caroline Co, VA, d. 1906; m. 13 Nov 1837 to William B Taylor, b. 1824, d. 1857. Their issue:

1. Lucy Taylor
2. Patrick Thomas Taylor
3. Margaret Susan Taylor
4. Anne E Taylor
5. Eleanor Taylor

Lucy Taylor, b. c. 1840 in Caroline Co, VA

Patrick Thomas Taylor, b. 14 May 1848 in Caroline Co, VA, d. 11 Mar 1914 of cardiovascular sclerosis in Richmond, VA; m. in 1877 in Wood, WV to Margaret (Maggie) Dorsey, b. 1854, d. 1945. They are buried in Mt Calvary Cemetery, Richmond, VA.

NOTE: Death certificate states he died 11 Mar 1914. His tombstone states the year as being 1913. Their issue:

1. Mary Madelilne (Mayme) Taylor, b. 1878, d. 1925; she married a Bunce
2. Loretta Taylor, b. 1879, d. 1886

3. Rose Lorraine Taylor, b. 1883, d. 1963

4. Lena Eugenia Taylor, b. 1885, d. 1973

5. Leo Baxter Taylor, b. 1889, d. 1955

6. Norbert Hudson Taylor, b. 14 Jun 1892, d. 18 Nov 1945 of lung cancer in Philadelphia, PA. He married Mary Woody. He is buried in Richmond, VA

7. Marguerite Ann Taylor, b. 1894, d. 1959

8. Claire Veronica Taylor, b. 1895, d. 1960

Margaret Susan Taylor, b. 6 Jan 1850 in Caroline Co, VA, d. 30 Oct 1923 of a cerebral hemorrhage in Richmond, VA; m. J Brightwell, b. ___________, d. ___________. They are buried in Oakwood Cemetery, Richmond, VA.

Anne E Taylor, b. 1853 in Caroline Co, VA, d. ___________

Eleanor Taylor, b. 13 Jul 1855 in Caroline Co, VA, d. 14 Feb 1931 of intestinal influenza in Richmond, VA; m. Junius J Farmer, b. ___________, d. ___________. They are buried in Oakwood Cemetery, Richmond, VA.

Page 267   Anna Rosalyn Taylor Landram, d. 4 Apr 2009; buried in Greenlawn Cemetery, Bowling Green, VA

Page 268   Vincent Rudolph Miller, d. 10 Dec 2012; buried in NC

Page 270   Ruby Taylor Pickett, d. 27 Dec 2010

Page 270   Edwin Lee Pickett, d. 7 Feb 2008

Page 270   Jean Taylor Kay, d. 11 May 2009; buried in Lakewood Cemetery, Bowling Green, VA

Page 272   John William Taylor, b. 6 Mar 1867, d. 6 Aug 1952; m. 8 Jan 1890 by Rev James H Marshall in Caroline Co, VA, to Florence Elizabeth (Bettie) Rouse, b. 16 Feb 1874, d. 16 Sep 1944. They are buried in Bethlehem Baptist Church Cemetery, Essex Co, VA. Their issue:

1. Jackson Hugh Taylor
2. Ruth L Taylor
3. Norma M Taylor
4. Grace Mae Taylor
5. Mabel F Taylor
6. Ena Viola (Peggy) Taylor

Jackson Hugh Taylor, b. 8 Nov 1890, d. 17 Apr 1936; m. 5 Jan 1918 to Mildred A Allen

Ruth L Taylor, b. 3 Mar 1893, m. 17 Apr 1936 to Willie S Taylor

Norma M Taylor, b. 1 Jun 1895, d. 1 Jun 1936

Grace Mae Taylor, b. 16 Oct 1897, d. 8 Oct 1978; m. 12 Apr 1922 to Harry L Brooks

Mabel F Taylor, b. 8 Oct 1899, d. 13 Dec 1988; m. (1) 8 Dec 1917 to Beale F Parker; m. (2) _____________ Howdershelt, b. _____________

Ena Viola (Peggy) Taylor, b. 24 Mar 1904, d. 4 May 1979; m. (1)

12 Jan 1933 to Herschel Culver; m. (2) 1 Jun 1939 to Sidney Eugene King, b. 22 Aug 1906, d. 24 Apr 2002. Peggy and Sidney moved to "The Willows" farm in 1945 where he established his studio and where all his famous works were painted. They are buried in Bethlehem Baptist Church Cemetery, Essex Co, VA.

Page 272   Margaret Ann Taylor, b. 1830, d. Oct 1878; m. 26 Dec 1846 to James H Marshall(Farmer and a Minister), b. 1830, d. ___________
Their issue:

1.   Rebecca Marshall, b. c. 1858
2.   Hudson Marshall, b. c. 1859
3.   C M (Female) Marshall, b. c. 1862
4.   William H Marshall, b. c. 1864
5.   Fanny Marshall, b. c. 1866
6.   Thomas J Marshall, b. c. 1868
7.   Ella Marshall, b. c. 1868

Lucy Myra Dillard Taylor

Alberta S Taylor & Berkley Muscoe Noel and James Liston Taylor

1800's Taylor family

This original photo was taken in 1895 of Oscar Taylor
and his second wife, Mary A. Lipscomb. Oscar was born
in Caroline County in 1850, one of six boys born to
William W. Taylor and Nancy Houston. His first wife
was Maria Vaughan. They were married Nov. 12, 1874
and later moved to West Point in King William County.
Mary was born in 1860, the daughter of Archie
Lipscomb. Mary had been married before to James R.
Prince of King and Queen County. Oscar and Mary
married after James R. Prince died and moved to
Emporia where both died before 1905.

1800's Taylor family

Jesse Taylor

The back side of Grandma and Grandpa Taylor's home

Grandma Taylor & Children

Myrtle Taylor & Kate Taylor

C O P Y

The following is a copy of a letter written by Frank L. Taylor (my grandfather) to his niece, Minnie Taylor, concerning the illness of his brother, James Liston Taylor:

Shumansville, Virginia

July 11th, 1934

Dear Minnie,

I received your letter and was sorry to hear of the illness of your father. I do wish I could come to see him but at present we are all sick and hardly able to wait on each other. I am suffering with rheumatism and can't get about without two sticks and sometimes they have to help me. The rest of the family seems to be in the dumps so there we are. I do hope that your father's condition will soon improve, do let me hear from him real often. As to his last resting place I never heard him say but I did understand from Clarence and his family that he wanted to be placed by the side of mother and father in the Family Burying Ground near Sparta but it doesn't matter where the body is buried if the soul is at peace with God. Now I will close by asking you to remember me to them one and all and write soon.

Your Uncle,

Frank L. Taylor

Letter written by Frank L Taylor dated July 11th, 1934

Marriage License

Virginia ___Caroline County___ _to-wit:_

To Any Person Licensed to Celebrate Marriages:

You are hereby authorized to join together in the Holy State of Matrimony, according to the rites and ceremonies of your Church or religious denomination, and the laws of the Commonwealth of Virginia,

___Clarence W. Reece___ *and* ___Alberta Taylor___

*Given under my hand, as Clerk of*___Circuit___ *Court of* ___Caroline___ *County (or City) this* ___19___ *day of* ___Dec.___ *19__25*

E. S. Cogswell, *Clerk*

Marriage Certificate
To be annexed to the License, required by Section 5074 of the Code of Virginia, 1919.

VIRGINIA: In the Clerk's Office of the ___Circuit___ *Court for the County (or City) of* ___Caroline___

Date of Marriage ___December 24th, 1925.___ *Place of Marriage* ___Richmond, Va.___

(FULL NAMES OF PARTIES)

___Clarence W. Reece___ *and* ___Alberta Taylor___

Age of Husband ___22___ years; Condition (single, widowed or divorced) ___single___

Age of Wife ___22___ years; Condition (single, widowed or divorced) ___single___

Race (White or Colored) ___White___

(PRESENT)

Husband's Place of Birth ___Caldwell Co. N.C.___ Mailing Address ___Point Eastern, Va.___

Wife's Place of Birth ___Caroline Co. Va.___ Mailing Address ___Lorne, Va.___

Names of Parents { Husband ___William Reece___ and ___Lola Reece___

Wife ___R. L. Taylor___ and ___Eva M. Taylor___

Occupation of Husband ___Sawmilling___

Given under my hand this ___19th___ *day of* ___December___ *, 19__25.*

E. S. Cogswell, *Clerk.*

Certificate of Time and Place of Marriage

I, _H. W. Landrum_, a _Minister_ of the _M. E._ Church, or religious order of that name, do certify that on the _24_ day of _Dec._, 19_25_, at _Ashland_, Virginia, under authority of the above License, I joined together in the Holy State of Matrimony the persons named and described therein. I qualified and gave bond according to law authorizing me to celebrate the rites of marriage in the County (or City) of _Franklin_, State of Virginia.

Given under my hand this _24_ day of _December_, 19_25_

H. W. Landrum

(Person who performs ceremony sign here.)

The Minister or other person celebrating a marriage is required, within thirty (30) days thereafter, to return the License and Certificate of the Clerk and his certificate of the time and place at which the marriage was celebrated to the Clerk who issued the License; failure to comply with these requirements of the law makes the Minister or other person celebrating the marriage liable to a fine of not less than ten nor more than twenty dollars for each offense (see Section 5074 of the Code of Virginia, 1919.

Marriage License of Clarence W Reece & Alberta Taylor

MARRIAGE LICENSE

Virginia, _Caroline County_ to wit:

To any Person Licensed to Celebrate Marriages:

You are hereby authorized to join together in the Holy State of Matrimony according to the rites and ceremonies of your Church, or religious denomination, and the laws of the Commonwealth of Virginia,

Burton Lewis Taylor

and _Anna Frawner_

Given under my hand, as Clerk of the _County_ Court of _Caroline_ this _11th_ day of _Nov._ _1903_

E. R. Coghill Clerk.

CERTIFICATE TO OBTAIN A MARRIAGE LICENSE

TO BE ANNEXED TO THE LICENSE, REQUIRED BY SECTION 2229 OF THE CODE OF VIRGINIA AS AMENDED BY ACT OF FEBRUARY 3, 1900.

Time of Marriage, _Nov. 12th 1903_
Place of Marriage, _Caroline Co. Va._
Full Names of Parties Married, _as above_
Color, _White_
Age of Husband, _56 years_
Age of Wife, _58 "_
Condition of Husband ~~(widowed or single or divorced)~~
Condition of Wife ~~(widowed or single or divorced)~~

Place of Husband's Birth, _Caroline Co. Va._
Place of Wife's Birth, _" "_
Place of Husband's Residence, _" "_
Place of Wife's Residence, _" "_
Names of Husband's Parents, _John and Myra Taylor_
Name of Wife's Parents, _H. and P. Seymour_
Occupation of Husband, _Farmer_

Given under my hand this _11th_ day of _Nov._ _1903_

E. R. Coghill Clerk

Certificate of Time and Place of Marriage.

I _James H. Marshall_, a Minister of the _Baptist_ Church, or religious order of that name, do certify that on the _12th_ day of _November 1903_, at _Plain View_, under authority of the above License, I united in Marriage the persons named and described therein.

Given under my hand this _12th_ day of _November 1903._

James H. Marshall.

☞ The Minister Celebrating a marriage is required within two months thereafter, to return the License to the Office of the Clerk who issued the same, with an endorsement thereon of the FACT of such marriage, and of the TIME and PLACE of celebrating the same.

Marriage License of Burton Lewis Taylor & Anna Frawner

CERTIFICATE OF DEATH
COMMONWEALTH OF VIRGINIA
DEPARTMENT OF HEALTH
BUREAU OF VITAL STATISTICS

Department of Commerce
Bureau of the Census

State File No. 18605
Registered No. 1924

1. PLACE OF DEATH

(a) County ______
Registration district No. ______ (For reg. use)

(b) Magisterial district ______

(c) City or town Richmond Va

(d) Name of hospital or institution ______ Memorial Hospital

(e) Length of stay in hosp. or inst. ______ In this community ______
(Specify whether years, months, or days)

(f) Is place of death within corporate limits? Yes

2. USUAL RESIDENCE OF DECEASED

(a) State ______

(b) County ______

(c) City or town Richmond Va

(d) Street No. 1506 McDonough St

(e) Is place of residence within corporate limits? Yes

(f) If foreign birth, how long in U. S. A? ______ Years

1. FULL NAME Alexander Mortimer Beasley

3. (c) Social security number ______ (Answer only if card is available)

5. Sex Male   6. Color or race White   6. (a) Single, married, widowed, divorced. Widowed

7. Name of husband or wife Virginia Taylor

Date of birth of deceased Oct 8, 1853
(Month by name) (Day) (Year)

4. Age: Years 86   Months   Days   If less than one day ______ hours ______ min.

8. Birthplace Caroline   Va
(City, town, or county)   (State or foreign country)

9. Usual occupation Farmer

10. Industry or business ______

12. Name Thomas H Beasley
13. Birthplace Caroline Va.
(City, town or county) (State or foreign country)

14. Maiden name Elizabeth F. Sawter Beasley
15. Birthplace Caroline Va.
(City, town or county) (State or foreign country)

16. (a) Informant's own signature Patient
(b) Address 1506 McDonough St.

17. (a) Burial, cremation, or removal? Burial
Hanover Co.
(b) Place ______ Date Feb. 2 1940
(Month by name) (Day) (Year)

18. Signature of funeral director E H Morrisett Hines
(b) Address 318 Cowardin Ave.

19. Filed Sept. 1, 1940
(Date received by reg.)
(Local, deputy, or sub-registrar's own signature)

MEDICAL CERTIFICATION

20. Date of death Aug. 31 1940 at 8:50
(Month by name) (Day) (Year) (Hour)

21. I hereby certify that I attended the deceased from Aug. 28 1940 to Aug 31 40; that I last saw h___ alive on Aug 31 1940; and that death occurred on the date and hour stated above.
Immediate cause of death Cerebral hemorrhage
Due to Hypertensive heart disease
Due to Arteriosclerosis
Other conditions ______
(Include pregnancy within 3 months of death)

Name of operation ______
Date of operation ______ Major findings: (a) of operations ______
(b) of autopsy ______

Duration ______

Physician
Underline the primary cause to which death should be charged statistically.

22. If death was due to external causes fill in the following:
(a) Accident, suicide, or homicide (specify) ______
(b) Date of occurrence ______
(c) Where did injury occur? ______
(City or town) (County) (State)
(d) Did injury occur in or about home, on farm, in industrial place, in public place? ______
(Specify type of place)
While at work? ______
(e) Means of injury ______

23. Signature M. J. Hoover M. D., Cor., or other
Address 1205 E Marshall
Date signed 8/7/40

6

1940

A. M. BEASLEY
A. M. Beasley, 86-year-old retired farmer, died Saturday at a local hospital. He is survived by five sons, Robert F. C. M., H. W., J. T. and A. E. Beasley. Funeral services will be held at 2 P. M. Monday at Morrisett's Funeral Home, 318 Cowardin Avenue, with burial at Wins Baptist Church in Hanover County.

Virgin T Taylor once belonged to Providence Bap Ch. Entry in "Minute Book" — VA T Beasley died Apr 1896

Certificate of Death for Alexander Mortimer Beasley.

Form V. S. No. 12—6-13-32—50M.

N. B.=WRITE PLAINLY, WITH UNFADING INK (WRITING FLUID). THIS IS A PERMANENT RECORD. EVERY ITEM OF INFORMATION SHOULD BE CAREFULLY SUPPLIED. AGE SHOULD BE STATED EXACTLY. PHYSICIANS SHOULD STATE THE CAUSE OF DEATH IN PLAIN TERMS, SO THAT IT MAY BE PROPERLY CLASSIFIED. EXACT STATEMENT OF OCCUPATION IS VERY IMPORTANT.

MARGIN RESERVED FOR BINDING

CERTIFICATE OF DEATH
COMMONWEALTH OF VIRGINIA
DEPARTMENT OF HEALTH
BUREAU OF VITAL STATISTICS

8808

1 PLACE OF DEATH
COUNTY OF Henrico
MAGISTERIAL DISTRICT OF
OR INC. TOWN OF
OR CITY OF Richmond

REGISTRATION DISTRICT No. ________ REGISTERED No. **976**
(TO BE INSERTED BY REGISTRAR) (FOR USE OF LOCAL REGISTRAR)
(No. 618 Albemarle St. ________ ST. ________ WARD)
(If death occurred in a hospital or other institution, give its NAME instead of street and number)

Length of residence in city or town where death occurred ____ yrs ____ mos ____ ds How long in U. S., if of foreign birth? ____ yrs ____ mos ____ ds

2 FULL NAME Edgar Taylor
(A) RESIDENCE. NO. 618 Albemarle St. ST. ________ WARD
(Usual place of abode) (If nonresident give city or town and State)

PERSONAL AND STATISTICAL PARTICULARS

3. SEX Male
4. COLOR OR RACE White
5. SINGLE, MARRIED, WIDOWED, OR DIVORCED (write the word) Married

5A. IF MARRIED, WIDOWED, OR DIVORCED HUSBAND OF (OR) WIFE OF Mary E. Taylor

6. DATE OF BIRTH (month, day, and year) Nov. 14th 1857

7. AGE Years 76 | Months | Days | IF LESS THAN 1 DAY, ____ HRS. OR ____ MIN.

OCCUPATION
8. TRADE, PROFESSION, OR PARTICULAR KIND OF WORK DONE, AS SPINNER, SAWYER, BOOKKEEPER, ETC. Retired Carpenter
9. INDUSTRY OR BUSINESS IN WHICH WORK WAS DONE, AS SILK MILL, SAW MILL, BANK, ETC.
10. DATE DECEASED LAST WORKED AT THIS OCCUPATION (month and year)
11. TOTAL TIME (YEARS) SPENT IN THIS OCCUPATION

12. BIRTHPLACE (city or town) Caroline Co., Va.
(State or country)

FATHER
13. NAME Wm. Woodford Taylor
14. BIRTHPLACE (city or town) Caroline Co., Va.
(State or country)

MOTHER
15. MAIDEN NAME Nancy Houston
16. BIRTHPLACE (city or town) Caroline Co., Va.
(State or country)

17. INFORMANT Mrs. Mary E. Taylor
(ADDRESS) 618 Albemarle St.

18. BURIAL, CREMATION, OR REMOVAL PLACE Caroline Co., Va. DATE Apr. 25/1934

19. UNDERTAKER Chas J Billups + Sons
(ADDRESS) Richmond, Va.

20. FILED April 25 1934 W. B. Foster Registrar.

MEDICAL CERTIFICATE OF DEATH

21. DATE OF DEATH (month, day, and year) April 23 1934

22. I HEREBY CERTIFY, THAT I ATTENDED DECEASED FROM April 20, 1934 TO April 22, 1934
I LAST SAW HIM ALIVE ON April 22, 1934, DEATH IS SAID TO HAVE OCCURRED ON THE DATE STATED ABOVE, AT 4:44 P M.
THE PRINCIPAL CAUSE OF DEATH AND RELATED CAUSES OF IMPORTANCE IN ORDER OF ONSET WERE AS FOLLOWS:

	Date of onset
Gen Arterio - Vascular - Renal with nephrosis	4/20/34

CONTRIBUTORY CAUSES OF IMPORTANCE NOT RELATED TO PRINCIPAL CAUSE Acute Bronchitis — 4/21/34

NAME OF OPERATION No DATE OF ____
WHAT TEST CONFIRMED DIAGNOSIS? Routine WAS THERE AN AUTOPSY? No

23. IF DEATH WAS DUE TO EXTERNAL CAUSES (VIOLENCE) FILL IN ALSO THE FOLLOWING:
ACCIDENT, SUICIDE, OR HOMICIDE? ____ DATE OF INJURY ____
WHERE DID INJURY OCCUR? (Specify city or town, county, and State)
SPECIFY WHETHER INJURY OCCURRED IN INDUSTRY, IN HOME, OR IN PUBLIC PLACE.
MANNER OF INJURY
NATURE OF INJURY

24. WAS DISEASE OR INJURY IN ANY WAY RELATED TO OCCUPATION OF DECEASED?
IF SO, SPECIFY

(SIGNED) Rush F Summers, M.D.
(ADDRESS) 211 W. Grace St.

Certificate of Death for Edgar Taylor.

H. D. V. S., Form No. 13, 200M.—5-15-12.

COMMONWEALTH OF VIRGINIA
STATE BOARD OF HEALTH
Bureau of Vital Statistics

CERTIFICATE OF DEATH

1. PLACE OF DEATH.

County of *Henrico*

District of ....

or
Inc. Town of ....

or
City of *Richmond* (No. *2606 E Grace* St. .... Ward)

File No. *6024*

Registered No. *566*

[If death occured in a Hospital or Institution give its NAME instead of street and number.]

2. FULL NAME *Patrick Thomas Taylor*

Residence In City ...... Yrs. ...... Mos. ...... Days ......

PERSONAL AND STATISTICAL PARTICULARS	MEDICAL CERTIFICATE OF DEATH

3. SEX *Male*   4. COLOR OR RACE *White*   5. SINGLE, MARRIED, WIDOWED, OR DIVORCED. (Write the word) *Married*

16. DATE OF DEATH *Mch* *16*, 191*4* (Month) (Day) (Year)

6. DATE OF BIRTH *May 14th*, 18*49* (Month) (Day) (Year)

17. I HEREBY CERTIFY, That I attended deceased from *Feb*, 191*1*, to *Mch 9*, 191*4* that I last saw h— alive on *Mch 8*, 191*4* and that death occurred, on the date stated above, at *5* m. The CAUSE OF DEATH★ was as follows:

7. AGE *65* yrs. ...... mos. ...... ds.   If LESS than 1 day, ... hrs. or ...... min.?

Cardio vascular sclerosis
Interstitial Nephritis chronic

8. OCCUPATION
(a) Trade, profession, or particular kind of work *Engineer*
(b) General nature of industry, business, or establishment in which employed (or employer)

many (Duration) ...... yrs. ...... mos. ...... ds.

9. BIRTHPLACE (State or Country) *Caroline Co. Virginia, —*

Contributory (SECONDARY)

(Duration) ...... yrs. ...... mos. ...... ds.

PARENTS

10. NAME OF FATHER *Wm Taylor*

(Signed) *Henry Leen* M. D.

11. BIRTHPLACE OF FATHER (State or Country) *Caroline Co Virginia*

Mch 11, 191*4* (Address) *205 W —*

12. MAIDEN NAME OF MOTHER *Mrs Mildred Taylor*

★State the DISEASE CAUSING DEATH, or, in deaths from VIOLENT CAUSES, state (1) MEANS OF INJURY; and (2) whether ACCIDENTAL, SUICIDAL or HOMICIDAL.

13. BIRTHPLACE OF MOTHER (State or Country) *Caroline Co. Virginia*

18. LENGTH OF RESIDENCE (For Hospitals, Institutions, Transients, or recent Residents) At place of death ...... yrs. ...... mos. ...... ds. In the State ...... yrs. ...... mos. ...... ds. Where was disease contracted, if not at place of death? ...... Former or usual Residence ......

14. THE ABOVE IS TRUE TO THE BEST OF MY KNOWLEDGE

(Informant) *Mrs P. T. Taylor* (Secondary)

(Address) *2606 E Grace St*

19. PLACE OF BURIAL OR REMOVAL. *Mt Calvary*   DATE OF BURIAL *Mch 13*, 191*4*

15. Filed *3/13*, 191*4* *J. F. Waller* LOCAL REGISTRAR

20. UNDERTAKER *H. A. Roden*   ADDRESS *City*

Certificate of Death for Patrick Thomas Taylor.

HVS-20010—150M—2.45

COMMONWEALTH OF PENNSYLVANIA
DEPARTMENT OF HEALTH
BUREAU OF VITAL STATISTICS

File No. *99888*

Primary Dist. No.

CERTIFICATE OF DEATH

Registered No. *22,467*

1. PLACE OF DEATH:
(a) County *Philadelphia*
(b) Township
(c) Borough
(d) City *Philadelphia*
(e) Name of hospital or institution *Temple University*
(If not in hospital or inst. write street number or location)
(f) Length of stay: In hospital or inst. ______ (g) In this community ______

2. USUAL RESIDENCE OF DECEASED:
(a) State *Penna* (b) County *Phila*
(c) City or town *Philadelphia*
(If outside city or town limits, write RURAL)
(d) Street No. *3550 North Broad St.*
(If rural give location)
(e) If citizen of foreign country, name country ______

3. (a) FULL NAME *Norbert H. Taylor*

3. (b) If U.S. Veteran, complete reverse side of certificate
3. (c) Social Security No. ______

4. Sex *Male* 5. Color or race *White* 6. (a) Single, widowed, married, divorced *Married*
6. (b) Name of husband or wife *Mary Woody*
6. (c) Age of husband or wife if alive ______ years
7. Birth date of deceased *June 14, 1892*
(Month) (Day) (Year)

8. AGE: Years *53* | Months *5* | Days *4* | If less than one day ______ hr. ______ min.

9. Birthplace *Richmond, Va.*
(City, town, or county) (State or foreign country)
10. Usual occupation *Export Tobacco Co*
11. Industry or business ______

MOTHER FATHER
12. Name *Patrick Taylor*
13. Birthplace *Virginia*
(City, town, or county) (State or foreign country)
14. Maiden name *Margaret Dorsey*
15. Birthplace *Maryland*
(City, town, or county) (State or foreign country)

16.(a) Informant's own signature *Alice T. Cherry*
(b) Address *Richmond, Va.*

17. (a) *Burial* (b) Date thereof *Nov. 21, 1945*
(Burial, cremation, or removal) (Month) (Day) (Year)
(c) Place *Richmond* County ______ State *Va.*

18. (a) Signature of funeral director *H. Robinson for*
(b) Address *A.H. Bair Co. Phila. Pa.*

19. (a) *11-18-45* (b) *Joseph A. Dowell*
(Date received local registrar) (Registrar's signature)

MEDICAL CERTIFICATION

20. Date of death: Month *Nov.* day *18*
year *1945* hour *12* minute *45 AM*

21. I hereby certify that I attended the deceased from *Nov. 1*, 19 *45* to *Nov. 18*, 19 *45*
that I last saw h *im* alive on *Nov. 18*, 19 *45*
and that death occurred on the date and hour stated above.

Immediate cause of death *Cancer of lung.*

Due to ______

Due to ______

Other conditions *Postoperative cardiac failure*
(Include pregnancy within 3 months of death)

Major findings:
Of operations ______
Of autopsy ______

DURATION

PHYSICIAN
Underline the cause to which death should be charged statistically.

22. If death was due to external causes, fill in the following:
(a) (Probably) Accident, suicide, or homicide (specify) ______
(b) Date of occurrence ______
(c) Where did injury occur? ______
(City or town) (County) (State)
(d) Did injury occur in or about home, on farm, in industrial place, in public place? ______
(Specify type of place)
While at work? ______ (e) Means of injury ______
23. Signature *Richard Say* (M. D. or other)
Address *Temple Univ. Hosp.* Date signed *11/18/45*

—10

Certificate of Death for Norbert H Taylor.

FORM NO. 12

CERTIFICATE OF DEATH
COMMONWEALTH OF VIRGINIA
BUREAU OF VITAL STATISTICS
STATE BOARD OF HEALTH

2369
24686

1 PLACE OF DEATH
COUNTY OF Henrico
MAGISTERIAL DISTRICT OF
OR
INC. TOWN OF
OR
CITY OF Richmond, Va.

REGISTRATION DISTRICT No.
(TO BE INSERTED BY REGISTRAR)
REGISTERED No.
(FOR USE OF LOCAL REGISTRAR)

(No. 821 Nicholson St.) WARD)
(If death occurred in a hospital or other institution, give its NAME instead of street and number)

2 FULL NAME Mrs. Margaret S. Brightwell
(A) RESIDENCE: No. 821 Nicholson St. ST. WARD.
(Usual place of abode) (If nonresident give city or town and State)
Length of residence in city or town where death occurred ___ yrs. ___ mos. ___ ds. How long in U. S., if of foreign birth? ___ yrs. ___ mos. ___ ds.

PERSONAL AND STATISTICAL PARTICULARS

3 SEX Female
4 COLOR OR RACE White
5 SINGLE, MARRIED, WIDOWED, OR DIVORCED (write the word) Married

5A IF MARRIED, WIDOWED, OR DIVORCED HUSBAND OF (OR) WIFE OF J. Brightwell

6 DATE OF BIRTH (MONTH, DAY, AND YEAR, WRITE NAME OF MONTH) January 6, 1850

7 AGE YEARS 73 MONTHS 9 DAYS 24 IF LESS THAN 1 DAY, ___ HRS. OR ___ MIN.

8 OCCUPATION OF DECEASED
(A) TRADE, PROFESSION, OR PARTICULAR KIND OF WORK
(B) GENERAL NATURE OF INDUSTRY, BUSINESS, OR ESTABLISHMENT IN WHICH EMPLOYED (OR EMPLOYER) none
(C) NAME OF EMPLOYER

9 BIRTHPLACE
(CITY OR TOWN) Caroline county
(STATE OR COUNTRY) Va.

PARENTS

10 NAME OF FATHER William B. Taylor
11 BIRTHPLACE OF FATHER
(CITY OR TOWN) Caroline county
(STATE OR COUNTRY) Va.

12 MAIDEN NAME OF MOTHER Mildred E. Taylor
13 BIRTHPLACE OF MOTHER
(CITY OR TOWN) Caroline county
(STATE OR COUNTRY) Va.

14 INFORMANT Mrs. J. J. Farmer
(ADDRESS) 701 N. 34 St.

15 FILED 10/30/23

MEDICAL CERTIFICATE OF DEATH

16 DATE OF DEATH (MONTH, DAY, AND YEAR, WRITE NAME OF MONTH) Oct 30- 1923

17 I HEREBY CERTIFY, THAT I ATTENDED DECEASED FROM Oct 17- 1923 TO Oct 29 1923
THAT I LAST SAW HER ALIVE ON Oct 29 1923
AND THAT DEATH OCCURRED, ON DATE STATED ABOVE, AT 7:00 A.M.
THE CAUSE OF DEATH* WAS AS FOLLOWS:
Cerebral Haemorrhage.

(DURATION) ___ YRS. ___ MOS. ___ DS.

CONTRIBUTORY (SECONDARY)

(DURATION) ___ YRS. ___ MOS. ___ DS.

18 WHERE WAS DISEASE CONTRACTED IF NOT AT PLACE OF DEATH?
DID AN OPERATION PRECEDE DEATH? no DATE OF
WAS THERE AN AUTOPSY? no
WHAT TEST CONFIRMED DIAGNOSIS?
(SIGNED) ___ M. D.
Oct 30 1923 (ADDRESS) 2702 E Broad St.
*State the DISEASE CAUSING DEATH, or in deaths from VIOLENT CAUSES, state (1) MEANS AND NATURE OF INJURY, and (2) whether ACCIDENTAL, SUICIDAL, or HOMICIDAL.

19 PLACE OF BURIAL, CREMATION, OR REMOVAL Oakwood
DATE OF BURIAL Nov. 1 1923

20 UNDERTAKER Chas. J. Billups,
ADDRESS Richmond, Virginia.

Certificate of Death for Mrs Margaret S Brightwell.

Certificate of Death for Elnora Farmer.

A FALLEN LIMB

A limb has fallen from the family tree.
I keep hearing a voice that says, "Grieve not for me.

Remember the best times, the laughter, the song.
The good life I lived while I was strong.

Continue my heritage, I'm counting on you.
Keep smiling and surely the sun will shine through.

My mind is at ease, my soul is at rest.
Remembering all, how I truly was blessed.

Continue traditions, no matter how small.
Go on with your life, don't worry about falls

I miss you all dearly, so keep up your chin.
Until the day comes we're together again."

Author Unknown

MILITARY SERVICE –
THOSE WHO SERVED—CORRECTIONS
& ADDITIONAL INFORMATION

Page 352   WAR OF 1812:

JOHN H SEAL – He served in the rank of PVT in CPT Thomas Hickman's Company from Caroline Co, VA, attached to the 9th VA Militia Regiment commanded by LTC Elisha Boyd in the defense of Norfolk during the period 3 Aug 1814 to 24 Sep 1814, and was discharged at Falmouth in Stafford Co. After his discharge, he was called up again when the British fleet occupied Tappahannock during 2-4 Dec 1814 and proceeded north 12 miles further up the Rappahannock River. He served this time from 3-9 Dec 1814 as a PVT in CPT Elliott Dejarnetts' Company of Infantry of the 30th VA Militia Regiment of Caroline County commanded by MAJ Reuben Tankersley. Serving with him was a PVT David Seal, probably his brother. For his military service, he was awarded a land bounty of 40 acres.

CIVIL WAR:

J Achilles Southworth should read "JOHN ACHILLES SOUTHWORTH" - John Achilles Southworth was born in 1807 in Caroline Co, VA. Family lore says he was born at White Chimneys near a tavern of the same name. He reportedly gave wonderful public political speeches while standing on a barrel in Bowling Green, VA. However, there is every indication that he never learned to read or write during his lifetime, but there is evidence that some of his children did. It could be said that his need for communication honed his oral skills.

He was born during the second half of the second term of the third president of the United States, Thomas Jefferson, a fellow Virginian. This was a pivotal time in the history of the country. The Revolutionary War had been over barely 20 years before. The Louisiana Purchase earlier had brought the need to explore the territory and understand what "we had bought". The Lewis and Clark expedition would have just concluded with their arrival back in St Louis just one year earlier on 23 Sep 1806. The word of a vast country of opportunity and danger beyond the Virginia Allegheny Mountains and the great Mississippi must have been quite the conversation among the farmers and merchants of Caroline County trying to scratch out a living.

Achilles did not come from a southern aristocracy or wealthy English gentry. He lived a hard life of commitment to honest but back-breaking labor to feed his family. Somewhere along the way he must have apprenticed to become a shoemaker. Interestingly, his future daughter-in-law, Mahala Cecil, was the daughter of a shoemaker, James B Cecil, of Caroline Co.

On 22 Dec 1830, Achilles married Catherine Mahala Seal, the second oldest daughter of John and Margaret Edmundson Seal also of Caroline. They had 15 children. Catherine preceded Achilles in death in 1872. His life spanned 67 years before his death on 8 Jun 1874. This life saw 15 presidents following the third president, Thomas Jefferson, and ending under the 18th president, Ulysses S Grant. During this time there were two wars, the War of 1812 in which he was too young to serve and the Civil War in which he did serve along with his two sons, Ira and Hugh. Achilles enlisted at age 54 on 23 Jul 1861 in Bowling Green, VA, under CPT Thomas R Thornton's Company of the Caroline Light Artillery of the Virginia Volunteers. Due to his age and skill, he was detailed to the Confederate States Clothing Depot in Richmond, VA, where he served as a shoemaker. His last recorded payroll receipt was for Sep 1864 which was the time that Petersburg was under siege as Grant was attempting to take Richmond from the south during the Richmond-Petersburg Campaign from Jun 1864 to Mar 1865, culminating with the surrender at Appomattox in Apr 1865.

The importance of his service cannot be underestimated. Anyone who has served in the ground forces of the military knows the importance of footwear. Next to a soldier's weapon, durable comfortable footwear was close to being his next most important need. Unfortunately for the south there was a shortage of shoes and often soldiers went barefooted until shoes were available.

Achilles and Catherine owned property as noted in a contract of sale to James Blanton whereby Achilles and his wife sold 61 acres in Caroline located a half mile below Oakley on the way to Newtown. In the last will and testament of Achilles, dated 24 Apr 1874, instructions to the executor were to sell the 77-3/4 acres where he resided to Robert W. Pitts and distribute the proceeds of the sale to his children. In 1856 there was a signed trust agreement that Catherine would share equally in the real and personal estate of John Seal, her father. In the trust she would have use of the property during her lifetime, but upon her death it would be divided equally among her children. Specifically in the document, Achilles was required to agree to the distribution to the children.

IRA SOUTHWORTH – Ira was the first born of Achilles and Catherine Southworth in 1832 in Caroline Co, VA. The 1860 Census lists Ira, at age 28, living with Thomas L James and his wife, Mary, in Caroline. Thomas was a coachmaker and Ira a blacksmith. It is likely since Ira cannot read or write at this age, he is working for James in the building and repair of coaches as a blacksmith. Ira's trade will be utilized by the Confederate Army in the coming Civil War.

Ira enlisted in the Civil War under CPT Thornton's Virginia Light Artillery. His earliest recorded enlistment was 23 Jul 1861. He was 19 and enlisted when the unit was formed in Bowling Green in Caroline Co. His enlistment date is the same as his father, Achilles, and his brother, Hugh, all serving in the same unit. One can only imagine the distress and concern of Catherine, his mother, knowing that her husband and two sons were going up the road together to Bowling Green and off to war. The three Southworths, like many Americans of the time and generations before them when called to defend their way of life, did so willingly without regard for sacrifice. They were not serving to protect slavery. There's was not a way of life that made slavery something important to defend. What was important was keeping a life of independence from forces they saw as putting that way of life in danger of loss.

Ira served as a blacksmith during the war. His skill in coachmaking must have been transferrable to making wheels and caissons for the Confederate artillery pieces. He was assigned to the defense of Richmond where he is listed initially as a laborer near the close of 1862, but served the remainder of the war as a blacksmith. In Feb 1863, he was near Drewery's Bluff, located 7 miles south of Richmond on the James River and important to the defense of Richmond by naval attack or support of Union ground forces. In Mar 1862, fortifications were improved and Ira participated in this effort. Since he was listed as being in the Richmond area in 1864, it is likely he was near to a number of failed attempts by the Union to take Drewery's Bluff and perhaps took part in the evacuation of Richmond and Petersburg in Apr 1865. In addition to Ira's duties of making wheels and horseshoes, some of his other duties were to repair wagons and artillery. The military blacksmith operated from a traveling forge when not at a central depot or supply point. This traveling blacksmith shop was loaded with hundreds of horseshoes, tools, coal, iron supplies, an anvil and a vice, in all about 1200 pounds.

After the war, Ira met and married Mahala Cecil 10 Jan 1867; she was 24 and he was 10 or 11 years older. Around this time, Ira was employed by Mr John Delaware Hutchinson to clear land near the village of India Neck in King & Queen Co. The newly married couple went to Indian Neck and lived in one of the Hutchinson's buildings. The 1870 census reports that they were living in New Town Township where Ira worked on a farm. They had one child, Achilles Lee Southworth, who was born 10 Feb 1875. The family moved permanently to Indian Neck in 1875 where Ira opened a blacksmith shop. The family kept their ties to Caroline and reportedly walked the nine miles to Shiloh Methodist Church for Sunday Services.

The family name change from Southworth to Southard has been attributed to Lee's Liberty Hall school teacher, Mr. Hutchinson. However, property tax receipts from the King & Queen Treasurer on the six acres of land owned in Indian Neck list him as Ira Southard as does a letter dated 1901, testifying to his service in the Civil War. This testimony was successful in that Mahala is listed on the King & Queen Co, VA, Confederate Pension Rolls as Mahala Southard. Ira had opened a general store in Indian Neck in the late 1800's. As he was unable to read or write, he may have been relying on Lee's ability to read and write. Ira died at Indian Neck in 1905 and is buried in the Seal-Barlow cemetery near Shumansville, VA, beside his wife, Mahala, who died in Indian Neck 22 Oct 1922.

Private George W Pitts

Captain Thomas Rowe Thornton's Company

Virginia Light Artillery

(Caroline Light Artillery)

CPT Thomas R Thornton organized the Caroline Light Artillery in June 1861 at Bowling Green in Caroline County, Virginia. The battery mustered into Confederate Service on July 23, 1861, at Camp Magruder near Richmond and disbanded on April 9, 1865, at Appomattox Courthouse. During this period, its roster contained the names of two hundred and forty-three men, most of whom were from Caroline County, VA. Twelve of these men made the supreme sacrifice and never returned home. An additional ten men were wounded.

After it participated in the South Carolina major engagement of Pocotaligo, the Caroline Light Artillery returned to Richmond and assigned to LTC Charles Edward Lightfoot's Battalion of Light Artillery. It spent the remainder of the war as part of the Richmond Defenses and was engaged in the battle of Drewry's Bluff (May 1864) near Richmond, and finally at Appomattox in 1865.

PVT George W Pitts, born in 1842, enlisted in the Caroline Light Artillery on February 11, 1863, in Bowling Green, VA. He is listed as present for duty on Muster Rolls 7, dated September 1, 1863 through 14, the last Muster Roll dated February 28, 1865. He participated in the major engagements at Drewry's Bluff and Appomattox. The battery last saw action when it reached Red Oak Church, several miles past Appomattox Courthouse, by noon of April 9, 1865, with forty men, eight horses, and two guns. Before formal surrender proceedings took place, LTC Lightfoot received a dispatch from Gen Lee giving the men the option of staying with the Army or leaving to join Gen Johnston in North Carolina. Lightfoot left the decision to the men. The Caroline Light Artillery voted to join Gen Johnston. The men spiked the two remaining guns and with Lightfoot started marching south. After marching 2-3 miles, they discovered they were surrounded. The men were then given the choice of formally surrendering to Union units in order to obtain paroles or of proceeding directly home. Thirty-two men of the Caroline Light Artillery decided to go directly home and "worked their way home as best they could". Eight men from the Caroline Light Artillery were paroled at Appomattox.

PVT George W Pitts made his way home and was paroled at Ashland, Virginia, on May 2, 1865. On September 23, 1869, he married Betty Chinault. He died October 1, 1892 (found dead in the road near Burke's Bridge, approximately seven miles east of Bowling Green, VA). His widow applied for pension in Caroline County on August 1, 1910, receiving $22.50 per year.

Barlow Benjamin +

2Co. G, 47 Virginia Inf'y.

(CONFEDERATE.)

Private Private

CARD NUMBERS.

1	5160 4627	18	
2	4745	19	
3	4830	20	
4	2653	21	
5	2771	22	
6		23	
7		24	
8		25	
9		26	
10		27	
11		28	
12		29	
13		30	
14		31	
15		32	
16		33	
17		34	

Number of medical cards herein ....

Number of personal papers herein ....

BOOK MARK: ....

See also ....

3—2566

Military Card for Barlow Benjamin.

Copy

THE CONFEDERATE STATES, Dr.

To *Benjamin F Barlow Deceased*

Co G 47 Va

C. S. Army.

	DOLLARS.	CTS.
For Monthly Pay, from , 186 to 186		
being months, days, at per month,		
Treasury Certificate		
No 7506		
Deduct, due		
Amount paid,	54	30

I certify, that I have endorsed this Payment on

Descriptive Roll.

RECEIVED, *Richmond* this 26 day of *August* 186 3 from *Major John Ambler* Quartermaster C. S. Army, the sum of

Fifty four $\frac{30}{100}$ Dollars,

being the amount, and in full of the above account.

WITNESS,

Wm J Grundy

Atty

[Signed Duplicates.]

Richmond, 186

Personally appeared before me, a

Co. ( ), Regt. Vols., and made oath

that he is without a descriptive roll or final statement, which it is impossible to obtain from his commanding officer, for the reason that his company is now

that the above account, amounting to $\frac{}{100}$ Dollars,

is correct; that he is not in debt to the Confederate States, and that he will present a statement of this payment to his commanding officer.

Military Pay for Benjamin F Barlow Deceased.

(Confederate.)

| Capt. Thornton's Company, | Va. |
| Light Artillery. | |

E. D. Barlow

Pvt { Capt. Thomas R. Thornton's Co.
(Caroline L. Art'y) Virginia Vols.

Appears on

Company Muster Roll

of the organization named above,

for *Nov & Dec*, 186 4.
dated Dec 31 1864

Enlisted:
When *April 13*, 1864.
Where *Bow Green*
By whom *Capt Thornton*
Period *war*

Last paid:
By whom *Capt King*
To what time *Oct 31*, 1864.

Present or absent *present*

Remarks:

Captain Thornton's Company Virginia Light Artillery (Caroline Light Artillery) was organized July 23, 1861. It served in Lightfoot's Battalion of Artillery, which was composed of independent companies.

Book mark:

Wm Potter

(642)   Copyist.

(Confederate.)

| Capt. Thornton's Company, | Va. |
| Light Artillery. | |

E. D. Barlow

Pvt { Capt. Thomas R. Thornton's Co.
(Caroline L. Art'y) Virginia Vols.

Appears on

Company Muster Roll

of the organization named above,

for *Jany & Feby*, 186 5.
dated Feby 28 1865

Enlisted:
When *April 13*, 1864.
Where *Bow Green*
By whom *Capt Thornton*
Period *war*

Last paid:
By whom *Capt King*
To what time *Oct 31*, 1864.

Present or absent *present*

Remarks:

Captain Thornton's Company Virginia Light Artillery (Caroline Light Artillery) was organized July 23, 1861. It served in Lightfoot's Battalion of Artillery, which was composed of independent companies.

Book mark:

Wm Potter

(642)   Copyist.

Military Cards for E D Barlow.

APPLICATION of Disabled Soldier, Sailor or Marine of the late Confederacy
Under Act of April 2, 1902, as amended.

I, *Edward D. Barlow* do hereby apply for a pension under the provisions of the act of the General Assembly of Virginia, appro[ved] April 2, 1902, as amended, entitled "An act to aid the citizens of Virginia who were disabled by wounds received during the war between the Sta[tes] while serving as soldiers, sailors, or marines of Virginia, and such [as] served during the said war as soldiers, sailors, or marines of Virginia, who are [dis]abled by disease contracted during the war, or by the infirmities of age * * * and providing penalties for violating the provisions of this act." [I] do solemnly swear that I am a citizen of the State of Virginia, and that I have been an actual resident of the said State for two years, and of the [city] or county of my present residence for one year next preceding the date of this application, and that I was a soldier (sailor or marine) of the Confeder[ate] States in the war between the States, and that I am now disabled, and that from the effects of such disability I am incapacitated from following [my] usual and ordinary occupation, or any other occupation for a livelihood; and that during the said war I was loyal and true to my duty, and never, [at] any time deserted my command or voluntarily abandoned my post of duty in the said service, and that by reason of such service and disability I [am] now entitled to receive a pension under the provisions of said act. And I do further swear that I do not hold any national, State, city or county of[fice] or position which pays me in salary or fees TWO HUNDRED ($200.00) dollars per annum; nor have I an income from any other employment [or] any source whatever which amounts to TWO HUNDRED ($200.00) dollars per annum; nor do I receive from any source whatever money or other me[ans] of support amounting in value to the sum of TWO HUNDRED ($200.00) dollars per annum; nor do I own in my own right, nor does any one hold in trust for my benefit or use, nor does my wife own, nor does any one hold in trust for my wife, estate or property, either real, personal, or mixed, ei[ther] in fee or for life, of the assessed value of SEVEN HUNDRED AND FIFTY ($750.00) dollars; provided, however, that a soldier, sailor or marine [who] is totally blind, or who lost a hand or a foot while in the discharge of his duty during the war shall be entitled to a pension, unless he or his [wife] has an estate of the assessed value of ONE THOUSAND ($1,000.00) dollars; provided, further, that a soldier, sailor or marine who has reached the [age] of eighty years shall be entitled to a pension unless he or his wife shall have an estate of the assessed value of FIFTEEN HUNDRED ($1,500.00) doll[ars] nor do I receive any aid or pension from any other State, or from the United States, or from any other source, and that I am not an inmate of any soldi[ers'] home and am without means of support, either direct or indirect; and I do further swear that the answers given to the following questions are true[.]

All questions must be answered fully—be explicit:

1. What is your name? *Edward D. Barlow*

2. What is your age? *Sixty six* years.

3. Where were you born? *Caroline Co. Virginia*

4. How long have you resided in Virginia? *All my life*

5. How long have you resided in the City or County of your present residence? *66* years.

6. In what branch of the service were you? *Artillery* *Lightford's Battalion* Regiment. Company.

7. Who were your immediate superior officers?
Colonel *Lightford*
Captain *Thornton*

8. When did you enter the service? *Entered April 1864*

9. Where did you enter the service? *Richmond*

10. When and why did you leave the service? *at the close of the war*

11. Where do you reside? If in a city, give street address.
Post-office
County of *Caroline* Virginia

12. Have you ever applied for a pension in Virginia before? If yes, why are you not drawing one at this time? *Yes, and did not apply for it again because I was told I could not get it unless I were sixty five years old.*

13. What is your usual and ordinary occupation for earning a livelihood? *farming*

14. Are you following such occupation or any other occupation or employment at this time? If yes, state the nature and extent of same. *no*

15. What is your annual income? $ *52*
NOTE—By income is meant the total gross receipts derived by you [from] all crops (whether sold or used) wages and other sources valued in doll[ars]

16. How much property do you own?
Real Estate $ *87 acres*
Personal Property $ *one cow*

17. What is the exact nature of your disability and the cause thereof? *Old age and general de[bility]*

18. Are you totally or partially incapacitated by such disability? *Partially*

19. Give the names and addresses of two comrades who served in the command with you during the war.
Name *W. J. Chiles*
Address *Kidds Fork*
Name *Robert Pitts*
Address *Kidds Fork*
See Certificate "B."

20. Is there a camp of Confederate Veterans in your city or county?

21. Give here any other information you may possess relating to your [service] or disability which will support the justice of your claim.

A signature made by X mark is not valid unless attested by a witness.

WITNESS *B. Fuller*

Edward D. (his X mark) Barlow (Signature of Applicant.)

I, *J. W. Green*, a Justice of the peace in and for the *county* of *Caroline* in the State of Virginia, do certify that the applicant whose name is signed to the foregoing application, personally [ap]peared before me in my aforesaid, having the aforesaid application read to him and fully explained, as well as the statements and answ[ers] therein made, the said applicant made oath before me that the said statements and answers are true.

Given under my hand this *6* day of *July* 1912

J. W. Green J.P.
Signature of Officer

Application of Disabled Soldier for Edward D Barlow.

(Confederate.)		(Confederate.)

Left card:

(Confederate.)

| Capt. Thornton's Company, | **Va.** |
| Light Artillery. | |

Robt Barlow

Pvt , { Capt. Thomas R. Thornton's Co.
{ (Caroline L. Art'y) Virginia Vols.

Appears on

Company Muster Roll

of the organization named above,

for _Sept & Oct_ , 1864
Dated Nov 12 1864

Enlisted:
When _Sept 13_ , 1862.
Where _Bowling Green_
By whom _Capt Thornton_
Period _war_

Last paid:
By whom _Capt King_
To what time _Aug 31_ , 1864.

Present or absent _present_

Remarks:

Captain Thornton's Company Virginia Light Artillery (Caroline Light Artillery) was organized July 28, 1861. It served in Lightfoot's Battalion of Artillery, which was composed of independent companies.

Book mark:

(642)

Wm Potter
Copyist.

Right card:

(Confederate.)

13 | Thornton Artillery | Va

Robert D. Barlow

Pvt Thornton Artillery Va.

Residence _Caroline Co._

Appears on a

Return

of paroles issued by L. C. Fowler, Pro. Mar., Ashland, Va.

Roll dated Hd. Qrs. Pro. M. Office, Ashland, Va., June 1, 1865.

Parole issued _May 1_ , 1865.
Occupation _Farmer_
Remarks

Number of roll:
1

J E Douglas
(661)
Copyist.

Military Cards for Robt Barlow & Robert D Barlow

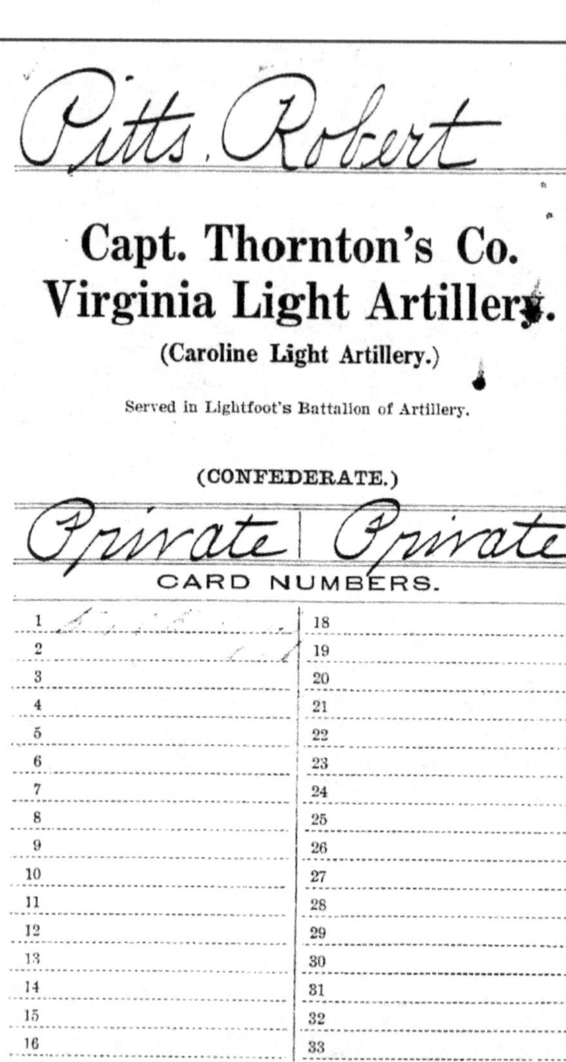

Military Card for Pitts Robert.

PENSIONERS now on the ROLL are NOT required to make new application, but must file annual certificate.

THIS APPLICATION must be filed with the Clerk of the Corporation or Circuit Court of Your City or County

(No application will be entertained not on the printed form.)

FORM No. 4

APPLICATION of a Disabled Soldier, Sailor or Marine of the Late Confederacy Under Act Approved February 28, 1918, as Amended by Act Approved March 10, 1920.

I, _Robert Pitts_ do hereby apply for a pension under the provisions of the act of the General Assembly of Virginia, approved March 10, 1920, amending an act approved February 28, 1918, relating to Confederate pensions."

I do solemnly swear that I am a citizen of the State of Virginia, and that I have been an actual resident of the said State for two years next preceding the date of this application, and that I was a soldier (sailor or marine) of the Confederate States in the war between the States, and that I am now disabled, and that from the effects of such disability I am incapacitated from following my usual and ordinary occupation, or any other occupation for a livelihood; and that during the said war I was loyal and true to my duty, and never, at any time deserted my command or voluntarily abandoned my post of duty in the said service, and that by reason of such service and disability I am now entitled to receive a pension under the provisions of said act. And I do further swear that I do not hold any national, State, city or county office or position which pays me in salary or fees Three Hundred ($300.00) dollars per annum; nor have I an income from any other employment or any source whatever which amounts to Three hundred ($300.00) dollars per annum; nor do I receive from any source whatever money or other means of support amounting in value to the sum of Three hundred ($300.00) dollars per annum; nor do I own in my own right, nor does any one hold in trust for my benefit or use, nor does my wife (who does any one hold in trust for my wife, estate or property, either real, personal, or mixed, either in fee or for life, of the assessed value of Two thousand ($2,000) dollars; nor do I receive any pension from any other State, or from the United States, or from any other source, and that I am not an inmate of any soldier's home and am without necessary means of support from any source, and that I do further swear that the answers given to the following questions are true:

All questions must be answered fully—be explicit.

1. What is your name? _Robert Pitts_

2. What is your age? _76_ years

3. Where were you born? _Caroline Co. Va._

4. How long have you resided in Virginia? _All my life_

5. How long have you resided in the City or County of your present residence? _76_ years

6. In what branch of the service were you? _Houstons Batten_ Regiment. _Eighth Va Battalion_ Company.

7. Who were your immediate superior officers?
Colonel _Hellyroot_
Captain _P. R. Shreder_

8. When did you enter the service? _October_ 186_5_

9. Where did you enter the service? _April 186_ _near Richmond_

10. When and why did you leave the service? _April 1865_

11. Where do you reside? If in a city, give street address.
Postoffice _Kidds Fork_
County of _Caroline_ Virginia

12. Have you ever applied for a pension in Virginia before? If so, why are you not drawing one at this time? _No_

13. What is your usual and ordinary occupation for earning a livelihood. _Farmer_

14. Are you following such occupation or any other occupation or employment at this time? If yes, state the nature and extent of same. _No_

15. What is your annual income? $ _450 00_
NOTE—By income is meant the total gross receipts derived by you from all crops (whether sold or used), wages and other sources valued in dollars.

16. How much property do you own?
Real Estate $ _1730_
Personal Property $ _1830_

17. What is the exact nature of your disability and the cause thereof? _Old age_

18. Are you totally or partially incapacitated by such disability? _Total_

19. Give the names and addresses of two comrades who served in the same command with you during the war.
Name _E. A. Barlow_
Address _Shumakersville_
Name _James R. Barlow_
Address
See Certificate "B."

20. Is there a camp of Confederate Veterans in your city or county? _Yes_

21. Give here any other information you may possess relating to your service or disability which will support the justice of your claim. _I was faithful in the discharge of my duty as a soldier_

A signature made by X mark is not valid unless attested by a witness.

WITNESS _E. N. Coghill_

Robert X Pitts
his mark
Signature of Applicant.

I, _E. R. Coghill Clerk Circuit Court_, in and for the _County_ of _Caroline_, in the State of Virginia, do certify that the applicant whose name is signed to the foregoing application, personally appeared before me in my _County_ aforesaid, having the aforesaid application read to him and fully explained, as well as the statements and answers therein made, the said applicant made oath before me that the said statements and answers are true.

Given under my hand this _7_ day of _September_, 19_22_ _E. R. Coghill Clerk_
Signature of Officer.

Application of a Disabled Soldier for Robert Pitts.

231

<u>Southworth, Achilles</u>

Capt. Thornton's Co.
Virginia Light Artillery.

(Caroline Light Artillery.)

Served in Lightfoot's Battalion of Artillery.

(CONFEDERATE.)

Private | *Private*

CARD NUMBERS.

#		#	
1	5105 1533	18	
2	1616	19	
3	1721	20	
4	1841	21	
5	1968	22	
6	2093	23	
7	2226	24	
8	2380	25	
9	2541	26	
10	2703	27	
11	2863	28	
12	3027	29	
13	8171	30	
14		31	
15		32	
16		33	
17		34	

Number of medical cards herein 0

Number of personal papers herein 0

BOOK MARK: ......

See also A. Southworth, 2 Batln Va Art,
Local Defense

3—2566

Military Card for Southworth Achilles.

| S | Capt. Thornton's Company,
Light Artillery. | **Va.** |

Archilles Southworth

Pvt. Capt. Thomas R. Thornton's Co.
(Caroline L. Art'y), Virginia Vols.

Appears on

Company Muster Roll

of the organization named above,

for Jany & Feby, 1862.
Dated Mch 11 1862

Enlisted:
When Feby 10, 1862.
Where Bowling Green
By whom Captain
Period The war

Last paid:
By whom
To what time ____, 186.

Present or absent Present
Remarks: Bounty Fifty dollars due

Captain Thornton's Company Virginia Light Artillery (Caroline Light Artillery) was organized July 28, 1861. It served in Lightfoot's Battalion of Artillery, which was composed of independent companies.

Book mark:

W. M. Potter

(642)   Copyist.

| S | Capt. Thornton's Company,
Light Artillery. | **Va.** |

Achilles Southworth

Pvt. Capt. Thomas R. Thornton's Co.
(Caroline L. Art'y), Virginia Vols.

Appears on

Company Muster Roll

of the organization named above,

for Mch & April, 1862.
Dated April 30 1862

Enlisted:
When Feby 10, 1862.
Where Caroline Co. Va.
By whom Captain
Period war

Last paid:
By whom Jos. M Brown Col Regt Va Vols
To what time Feby 28, 1862.

Present or absent Present
Remarks: At work

Captain Thornton's Company Virginia Light Artillery (Caroline Light Artillery) was organized July 28, 1861. It served in Lightfoot's Battalion of Artillery, which was composed of independent companies.

Book mark:

W. M. Potter

(642)   Copyist.

| S | Capt. Thornton's Company,
Light Artillery. | **Va.** |

Achilles Southworth

Pvt. Capt. Thomas R. Thornton's Co.
(Caroline L. Art'y), Virginia Vols.

Appears on

Company Muster Roll

of the organization named above,

for May & June, 1862.
Dated July 23 1862

Enlisted:
When Feby 10, 1862.
Where Bowling Green Va.
By whom Thos R Thornton
Period war

Last paid:
By whom Maj E Walke
To what time April 30, 186.

Present or absent present
Remarks:

Captain Thornton's Company Virginia Light Artillery (Caroline Light Artillery) was organized July 28, 1861. It served in Lightfoot's Battalion of Artillery, which was composed of independent companies.

Book mark:

W. M. Potter

(642)   Copyist.

Military Cards for Achilles Southworth.

(CONFEDERATE.)

S   Caroline Art.   Va.

A. Southworth

Appears on a

Receipt Roll

for extra duty pay of detailed shoemakers; received of Major R. P. Waller, Quartermaster, C. S. Army, Richmond, Virginia.

Roll dated Not dated ____, 186.

Date Feb. 9, 1863.
Services rendered Making 24 prs. shoes

Amount, $8.40
Signature A. his X mark Southworth
Remarks:

Book mark:

J. Cary

(658)   Copyist.

(CONFEDERATE)

A Southworth

Appears on a
RECEIPT ROLL
for pay
for Feb 9, 1863.

Date Feb 9, 1863.
Occupation Detailed shoemaker

PERIOD OF SERVICE:
From ____, 186.
To ____, 186.
Months
Days

Rate of pay
Signature
Remarks: Wit. G. F. Sinton

Roll No. 2972

SIMPSON

Copyist.

(CONFEDERATE)

A. Southworth

Appears on a
RECEIPT ROLL
for pay
for Feb. 9, 1863.

Date Feb. 9, 1863.
Occupation Detailed shoemaker

PERIOD OF SERVICE:
From ____, 186.
To ____, 186.
Months
Days

Rate of pay
Signature
Remarks: Wit. G. F. Sinton

Roll No. 2972

SIMPSON

Copyist.

Military Cards for A Southworth.

Capt. Thornton's Company, Va.
Light Artillery.

Achª Southworth
Pvt, Capt. Thomas R. Thornton's Co. (Caroline L. Art'y) Virginia Vols.

Appears on

Company Muster Roll

of the organization named above,

for _Nov & Dec_, 186 3.
Dated Jany 15 1864

Enlisted:
When _July 23_, 186_
Where _Bowling Green_
By whom _Capt Thornton_
Period _war_

Last paid:
By whom
To what time , 186 .

Present or absent _absent_
Remarks: _Detailed Dec 8, 1862 in Go. Clothing dept by order Secty war_

Captain Thornton's Company Virginia Light Artillery (Caroline Light Artillery) was organized July 23, 1861. It served in Lightfoot's Battalion of Artillery, which was composed of independent companies.

Book mark:

(842) W. H. Potter, Copyist.

(CONFEDERATE)
Thornton's Co 2 A.

A Southworth
Pvt, Caroline Arty

Appears on a
RECEIPT ROLL
for pay
for _Richmond Va_, 186 .
Date Dec 31, 186 3.
Occupation Shoemaker

PERIOD OF SERVICE:
From Dec 1, 186 3.
To Dec 31, 186 3.
Months
Days 25

Rate of pay $3. a day
Signature by X
Remarks:
5 days absent

Roll No. 135

HOOD
Copyist.

(CONFEDERATE)
Thornton's Co 2 A.

A Southworth
Pvt., Carolina Arty

Appears on a
RECEIPT ROLL
for pay
for _Richmond Va_, 186 .
Date _Jan 31_, 186 4.
Occupation Shoemaker

PERIOD OF SERVICE:
From Jan 1, 186 4.
To Jan 31, 186 4.
Months
Days 30

Rate of pay $3. a day
Signature by X
Remarks:
1 day absent

Roll No. 152

HOOD
Copyist.

Military Cards for Ach Southworth/A Southworth.

THE CONFEDERATE STATES, Dr.

To *A Southworth*

Carolina Arty "C. S. Army.

	DOLLARS.	CTS.
For Monthly Pay, from *Feby 2 8* 186*3* to *Apr 3 0* 186*3* being *2* months, days, at $ *1 2* per month,	24	
Detailed with Maj Waller		
Deduct, due		
A N Va		
Amount paid,	24	

I certify, that I have endorsed this Payment on *Southworths* Descriptive Roll.

John Ambler
Maj

RECEIVED, *Richmond* this *2* day of *May* 186*3* from *Maj John Ambler* Quartermaster C. S. Army, the sum of *Twenty four* ‾‾ Dollars, being the amount, and in full of the above account.

WITNESS, *T Moblitzee*

[Signed Duplicates.]

A × Southworth
mark

Military Pay for A Southworth.

Southworth, Hugh

Co. E, 30 Virginia Inf'y.

(CONFEDERATE.)

Private Private

CARD NUMBERS.

1		18	
2		19	
3		20	
4		21	
5		22	
6		23	
7		24	
8		25	
9		26	
10		27	
11		28	
12		29	
13		30	
14		31	
15		32	
16		33	
17		34	

Number of medical cards herein ....

Number of personal papers herein ....

BOOK MARK: ....

See also *Capt. Thornton's Co Va Lt. Art*

Military Card for Southworth Hugh.

Military Cards for Hugh Southworth.

(CONFEDERATE.)

S. | 30 | Va.

Hugh Southworth,

Pvt ____, Co. E, 30 Reg't Virginia Inf.

Appears on

Company Muster Roll

of the organization named above,

for *Mch and Apr*, 186 4

dated Apl. 30. 1864.

Enlisted:

When *July 23*, 186 1.

Where *Caroline*

By whom *Capt Thornton,*

Period *3 yrs.*

Last paid:

By whom _______________

To what time _______________, 186 .

Present or absent *Present,*

Remarks: *Transferred from Capt Thornton's Light Arty Vols.*

The 30th Regiment Virginia Infantry was organized June 13, 1861, and accepted into the service of the Confederate States July 1, 1861, with ten companies. Captain Green's Company was transferred to the 47th Regiment Virginia Infantry in July, 1861, and became Company A of that organization. Captain Tayloe's Independent Company Virginia Infantry was assigned to this regiment in July, 1861, and became Company K. (1st) Company I was exchanged in September, 1861, for (2d) Company I, 47th Regiment Virginia Infantry. The regiment was reorganized in April, 1862.

Book mark: _______________

W. Harr Scott,

(642) Copyist.

Military Card for Hugh Southworth.

Southworth Ira

Capt. Thornton's Co.
Virginia Light Artillery.

(Caroline Light Artillery.)

Served in Lightfoot's Battalion of Artillery.

(CONFEDERATE.)

Private | Private

CARD NUMBERS.

1	5105 1305	18	
2	1484	19	
3	1507	20	
4	1614	21	
5	1719	22	
6	1839	23	
7	1966	24	
8	2092	25	
9	2224	26	
10	2378	27	
11	2539	28	
12	2701	29	
13	2861	30	
14	3025	31	
15	3170	32	
16		33	
17		34	

Number of medical cards herein 0

Number of personal papers herein 0

BOOK MARK: ________________________

See also ________________________

3—2566

Military Card for Southworth Ira.

(Confederate.)
Capt. Thornton's Company, | **Va.**
Light Artillery.

Ira Southworth

Pvt. | Capt. Thomas R. Thornton's Co.
(Caroline L. Art'y), Virginia Vols.

Appears on

Company Muster Roll

of the organization named above,

for July & Aug, 186 3
Dated Sept 1 1863

Enlisted:
When July 23, 186 1.
Where Bowling Green
By whom Capt Thornton
Period war

Last paid:
By whom Capt King
To what time June 30, 186 3

Present or absent Present

Remarks:

Captain Thornton's Company Virginia Light Artillery (Caroline Light Artillery) was organized July 28, 1861. It served in Lightfoot's Battalion of Artillery, which was composed of independent companies.

Book mark:

(642) Copyist.

(CONFEDERATE.)

Capt. Thornton's Co.
Lt. Arty | Va.

Ira Southworth

Pvt., Caroline Lt. Arty.

Appears on a

ROLL

of non-commissioned officers and
privates employed on extra duty
at Cp. Near Richmond
during month of Feb, 186 4.

By whose order employed

Nature of service Blk. Smith

TERM OF SERVICE:
From Feb 1, 1864.
To Feb 29, 186 4.

Remarks:

Roll No.

Copyist.

(Confederate.)
Capt. Thornton's Company, | **Va.**
Light Artillery.

Ira Southworth

Pvt., | Capt. Thomas R. Thornton's Co.
(Caroline L. Art'y) Virginia Vols.

Appears on

Company Muster Roll

of the organization named above,

for Jan & Feb, 1865.
Dated Feb. 28, 1865.

Enlisted:
When July 23, 186 1.
Where Bow Green
By whom Capt Thornton
Period War

Last paid:
By whom Capt. King
To what time Oct. 31, 186 4

Present or absent Present
Remarks: Blacksmith

Captain Thornton's Company Virginia Light Artillery (Caroline Light Artillery) was organized July 23, 1861. It served in Lightfoot's Battalion of Artillery, which was composed of independent companies.

Book mark:

(642) Copyist.

Military Cards of Ira Southworth.

SGT Ian James McHugh

CPL Quinn Michael McHugh

Page 360   SPANISH AMERICAN WAR:

Robert Bernard Covington	PVT	Co C, 3d Rgmt, VA Inf
Francis Joseph Lochboehler		
Andrew Christian Taylor Sr		

Page 360   WORLD WAR I:

Eddie Shephard Barlow	PVT	USA
Edgar Allen Barlow	SGM	USA
Frank Martin Barlow	PVT	USA
Willard Bradford Barlow		USA
James Earl Driscoll Sr	CPL	USA
Strother William Lewis Sr	E2/C	USN
Frederick Payne Pavy Sr	SGT	USA
Joseph Clifton Pavy	USMC	
Carroll Floyd Pitts	F1/C	USN
Aubrey Leslie Southworth	PVT	USA
Leonard Street Southworth	PVT	USA
George Welford Taylor		USA
*Harry Mack Taylor	PFC	USA, Co C, 26th Inf
Julius Vernon Tuck	SGT	USA

Page 360   WORLD WAR II:

William Claiborne Ancarrow Jr	PFC	ARMY AF
Ennis Bradford Barlow	PFC	USA
Frances Josephine Barlow	Y1/C	WAVES
Joseph Alexander Barlow Jr	PFC	VA RESERVE MILITIA (MINUTEMEN)
*Joseph Eddie Barlow	MM3/C	USN

Lewis Walter Barlow Jr	PVT	USA
Ralph Linwood Barlow	BM3/C	USN
*Raymond Wesley Barlow	PVT	ARMY AF
William Bradford Barlow	PFC	USA
Clarence Garnett Beazley	PVT	USA
Edward Eustis Beazley	PVT	USA
Robert Carroll Beazley Sr	SSG	ARMY AF
Ross Harris Beazley	PVT	USA
Thomas Haywood Beazley	SGT	USA
Willard Earl Beazley	PFC	ARMY AF
William Edwin Beazley	SGT	USA
Olney Alfred Brawner		USN
John Edward Brooks	S2/C	USN
Ryland Hewlett Brooks	SGT	USA
Robert Edward Buchan		
Ralph Chance Jr		USN
Roy Davis Chinault	CPL	ARMY AF
Harry Francis Claytor		USA
Roy Lee Claytor		USN
Robert Douglas Cooper	SGT	USA
James Donald Covington		USA
John Chastine Covington		USA
Robert Beverly Covington	PFC	USA
Willing Bernard Covington	SSG	USMC
Henry Douglas Crowe	PFC	USA
James H Crowe		USA
Jackson Howard Crowell	PVT	USA
John H Crowell	PVT	USA
Willard Morris Crowell Jr	PVT	USA
James Earl Driscoll Jr	LTC	ARMY AF
James Alexander Dyson Sr		USN
Arthur (Junior) Farmer Jr	PFC	USMC
Willard Jasper Farmer	SGT	USA

Donald Carl Gatewood		USCG
Lewis Michael Gracik	T/5	ARMY AF
Elwood B Harmon		USN
Cephas Sale Haynes	PFC	USMC
*Thomas Raynard Hobson Sr	CPO	USN (Buried at Sea)
Elizabeth Yarbrough Taylor Jones	SGT	WAAF
Burleigh Trice Kay Sr	PFC	USA
James Burley Kelley	PFC	USA
Joseph A Lamont LTC		ARMY AF
Melvin Daniel Loving	SSG	ARMY AF
Wilbur Foster Loving	S1/C	USN
Joseph Bernard Matthews	T/5	ARMY AF
Mary Elizabeth Pavy Noles	PVT	WAC
Henry Joel (Mickey) Owen	SSG	USA
Clarence Archibald Bryce Pavy		SN
Cloyd Franklin Pavy		
Frederick Payne Pavy Jr		USN
James Samuel Pavy	PVT	USA
John Webb Pavy	PVT	USA
Joseph Clifton Pavy		USA
Ryland Milton Pavy Sr		USA
Thomas Edward Pavy	E-6	USN
Carroll Lawrence (Billy) Pitts		USN
Clyde L Pitts		USA
Edward Dawson Pitts	COX	USN
Franklin Dew Pitts	1LT	USMC
George Wilbur Pitts	S1/C	USN
Girtie Pitts		ARMY AF
Harry Franklin Pitts	S1/C	USN
*Joseph Lennon Pitts Jr	F1/C	USN
L F Pitts		USN
Marvin Warren Pitts	SSG	USA
Moody Clifton Pitts		USA

Otho Nelson (Son) Pitts	CM3	USN
Robert Otto (Robbie) Pitts		USA
Robert Wilson Pitts	2LT	USA
Robert Woodford (Dick) Pitts	S2/C	USN
Walter Dabney Priddy	SSG	USA
George Walker Pugh	SSG	USA
Edward Hewitt Reed	MM2/C	USN
John Rohs Jr	CPL	USMC
Clarence Burton Satterwhite		USA
Frank Benjamin Satterwhite		USA
Herell Curtis Satterwhite	PVT	USA
Percy Franklin Satterwhite	CPL	USA
Manley Weldon (Pete) Selph	CPT	ARMY AF
Aubrey Bernard Southworth		USA
*Jesse Willard Southworth	T/SGT	ARMY AF
John Wesley (Boots) Southworth	PFC	USA
Ray Carlton Southworth	SSG	ARMY AF
Willard Franklin (Ned) Southworth	FN	USN
Willard Jasper Southworth	SGT	USA
Herbert Adam Spayd		ARMY AF
George U (Bucky) Swain		USN
Andrew Christian Taylor Jr		USN
Charles Lloyd Taylor	SGT	USA
Floyd S Taylor		USA
Grayson Evans Taylor	SGT	USA
Henry Herbert Taylor	PFC	USA
Hugh Walker Taylor		USN
Irving Muscoe Taylor	T4/C	ARMY AF
Manley Dillard Taylor	CPL	USA
Preston Harvey Taylor	T5/C	ARMY AF
Richard Edward Taylor	GM 3/C	USN
Robert James Taylor		USN
Welford Daring Taylor		USA

Thomas Douglas Thomas	PFC	USA
Thomas Leonard (Nip) Tolley	SGT	USA
Stephen Andrew Tomicheck	CM 3/C	SEABEES
Clyde Everette Tuck	MOMM 3/C	USN
Joseph Earl Walton Sr		USN
William Edward Watts	PFC	USA
Francis Wade Weymouth		USN
Malcolm Bray Young	Y3/C	USN
Robert Edward Young	F2/C	USN
Thomas Edward Young	S2/C	USN

Page 363   KOREAN WAR:

Spencer Allen		USA
Clarence Ray Barlow	CPL	USA
Ross Harris Beazley		USA
Thomas David Brooks		USAF
James Harold Crowe		USA
Winston Clayton Crowe Sr		USA
Milton Grey (Billy) Farmer		USN
Joseph James Hartman	PFC	USA
Burleigh Trice Kay Sr	PFC	USA
Robert Lee Langford	CPL	USA
Strother William (Ted) Lewis Jr	SSG	USA
*Charles Raymond Loving	CPL	USA
James Edward Madison Jr	ABM 3/C	USN
Clinton Edward Pavy		USA
George Robert (Franklin) Pavy	S2/C	USN
John James Pavy Sr	CPO	USN
Roger Raymond Pavy	PFC	USA
Thomas Edward Pavy	E-6	USN
Albert Lee Pitts	CPL	USMC

Charles Eugene Pitts	SFC	USA
Charles Julian Pitts Sr	MM 3/C	USN
Edward Dawson Pitts	SFC	USA
William Russell Pitts	CPL	USA
James W Reed	MSG	USA
Ulysses Vilmon Selph Jr	CPL	USA
Ray Carlton Southworth	SSG	USAF
James Monroe Taylor		USA
William Gordon Taylor	CPL	USA
Wilbert Lloyd Whittaker	SGT	USA
James William (Corky) Young	PFC	USA

Page 363   VIETNAM WAR:

Richard Barlow	PO 2/C	USN
Harold Wade Beazley Sr	PO 2/C	USN
Edward Nelson Bowles	SFC	USA
Clarence Everett (Johnny) Brown		USA
Julian Roy Carter Jr	SP4	USA
Earl Chilton	MSG	USAF
Joseph Anthony Chimielewski Sr	SFC	USA
William Rundahl Coleman	DK2	USN
Claude Grayson Crisp		USAF
Thomas Anthony Dunnavant	SEA	USN
Ronald Elroy Holland	COMTEC	USN
Dennis Calvin Johnson		USN
Robert Lee Johnson		USA
Burleigh Trice Kay Jr		USA
Glen Curtis Mitchell	SGT	USAF
Franklin Delano Pauley	SFC	USA
Ryland Milton Pavy Jr		USA
David Smith Pitts	CPT	USAF

Edward Dawson Pitts	SFC	USA
James Norman Pitts	SGT	USA
Leslie Wayne Pitts		USA
Moody Clifton (Dick) Pitts Jr	SP4	USA
Ronald Wilbur Pitts	SP5	USA
Ruth Evelyn Pitts	SFC	WAC
Randolph F Satterwhite Sr		USA
George Herbert Spayd	PVT	USA
Jack Adam Spayd	TMC	USN
Douglas Earl Taylor Jr		USA
Robert James Taylor	CPO	USN
George Bryant White	CPT	USA
Gerald Lynn Wilcox	PO 2/C	USN
Arthur Herman Witmeyer	SGT	USA

Page 364   AFGHANISTAN/IRAQ

Atwell Burruss (Nick) Byrd	SSG	USA
Ashley Barlow Gray	1SGT	USMC
Roger Krause	SFC	USA
Edward William Lewis	CPT	USA
Ian James McHugh	SGT	USMC
Quinn Michael McHugh	CPL	USMC
Daniel Alan Melson	E-4	USAF
John Wayne Pitts Sr	1SGT	USA
Thomas Lee Pitts Jr	CM 1/C	SEABEES

Page 364   OTHERS WHO SERVED IN THE MILILARY SERVICE:

| Harris Gibson Allen | SP5 | USA |
| Everett William Andrews Jr | | USN |

Joseph Armistead		
Robert Owen Ayers Sr		USA
Anthony Earl Barlow	SP4	USA
Edward Dawson Barlow	SP5	USA
William Edward Barlow		USAF
Stephen Mitchell Bass	SGT	USAF
Thomas Warren Bass	CPO	USCG
Robert Carroll Beazley Jr	SP5	USA
Jackie Lee Bowles	SGT	USA
Garland Eugene Burnett		USA
Joseph Anthony Chimielewski Jr	SSG	USA
Dennis Carroll Chinault	MAJ	USMC
William Arthur Claytor Jr	SGT	USAF
David Peck Codington	CPT (CHAP)	USA
William Hyter Covington		USA
James Bryan Crisp		USCG
William Joseph Crisp		USN
Harvey Lewis Crowe Sr		USAF
Winston Clayton Crowe Jr		USA
Roger Carlton Gatewood	CPT	USAF
Charles Lewis Hagerty		USA
Elwood B Harmon	MSG	AIR NATIONAL GUARD
James Michael Hartman	SKSS	USN
Joseph Carl Hartman III	SKSS	USN
Thomas Anthony (Tony) Hartman	PO 1/C	USN
Hunter Cape Houston		USN
Arthur Ronald Johnson		
Matthew Wayne Johnson		USMC
James Burley Kelley	PFC	USA
Floyd Grayson Moore	SSG	USAF
Winfred Hampton (Buddy) Moore		USA
James Henry Owen	PFC	USA
Anita Carole Pavy	TSGT	USAF

John James Pavy Jr	CMSGT	USAF
John James Pavy Sr	MMC	USN
Donald James Pitts		USA
Donald Lee Pitts	SGT	USMC
George William Pitts Jr	CWO3	USCG
Howard Fernando Pitts	PVT	USA
James Robert Pitts Jr	P1-3	USN
Robert Wilton Pitts	2LT	USA
Robert Woodford (Dick) Pitts	PFC	USA
Stuart Tyler Pitts	SP5	USA
Robert Warren Reece	SSG	USAF
John Alton (Jerry) Reed		USN
Mitchell McRae Reed	SCH	USN
Richard James Spayd		USAF
Brad Stadelmeier	CPT	USMC
Jack Perry Taylor	EM 2/C	USN
John Michael Taylor		USAF
Kenneth Allen Taylor		USA
Raymond Lewis Taylor	T/SGT	USAF
Richard Monroe Taylor Jr	SP4	USA
Stuart Lee Taylor	A1/C	USAF
Warren Franklin Taylor	SP4	USA
William Randolph Taylor	PO 3/C	USN
Wirt Leon Taylor	CPL	USA
Woodford David Taylor Jr		USN
Calvin Fitzhugh Thornton Jr		USN
Maurice Franklin (Billy) Truslow	SSG	USAF
Clyde Everett Tuck Jr	PFC	USA
Donald Carl Young		USA
James William (Corky) Young		USA
Ronald Leary Young	SSG	USAF

*KIA (Killed In Action)

NOTES

The following information on births, marriages and deaths for the SEAL (SEALE), BARLOW, PITTS, SOUTHWORTH, TAYLOR, BOOK III, book was received too late to be included before the book was mailed to the publishers:

BARLOW FAMILY SECTION:

Page 104	Wilbon Newell Brown Bates, d. 3 Jan 2020. She was the daughter of Edith Covington Brown and is buried in Alabama.
Page 134	Issue of John Bradford Thomas and Jennifer Waguespack Thomas: Liam Allen Thomas, b. 18 May 2020 (Adopted)
Page 160 Page 186	Issue of Andrew Thomas Satterwhite and Kendall Barlow Satterwhite: Chilton Andrew Satterwhite, b. 28 May 2020
Page 199	Clarice Barlow Waddill, d. 13 Apr 2020. She was the daughter of Eddie Shepherd Barlow and widow of James Ray Waddill.

Issue of Taylor Dawn Schafer and Zachary Cordell Weaver, b. 15 Jul 1997:

Asher Vincent Weaver, b. 30 May 2019. He is the great-grandson of Maxine Taylor Pauley Miller.

Issue of Kristen Taylor Kraynak and Ian Christopher Kraynak:

Wrenley Bay Kraynak, b. 22 Jun 2015 (Adopted 20 Dec 2019). She is the great-granddaughter of Manley Dillard Taylor Sr.

Michael Lee Gatewood, d. 29 Apr 2020 (Cancer). He was the son of Ray Gatewood and Rae Covington Gatewood. He was cremated and his ashes are buried in Austin, TX.

James Edward Madison Jr, d. 9 Jul 2020 of cancer. He was the son of Elizabeth (Bessie) Taylor Madison and James Edward Madison Sr and the husband of Jane Barlow Madison. He is buried in Lakewood Cemetery, Bowling Green, VA.

Julia Taylor Lumpkin, d. 11 Aug 2020. She was the daughter of Frank Manley Taylor and Hausie Wharton Taylor and the wife of Willard Hazel Lumpkin. She is buried in Shiloh Baptist Church Cemetery, King George, VA.

PITTS FAMILY SECTION:

Page 46   Jean Marie Pitts, d. Nov 2019. She was the daughter of Joseph Lennon Pitts and Addie Lewis Pitts.

Page 57   Marvin Warren Pitts III, d. 25 May 2020. He was the grandson of Marvin Warren Pitts Sr and Lottie Garnett Pitts. He is buried in Mt Hermon Baptist Church Cemetery, Shumansville, VA.

Page 60   Cecil Satterwhite, d. 13 Jun 2019. He is the son of Curtis and Hazel Satterwhite and is buried in Westhampton Memorial Park, Richmond, VA.

PITTS & TAYLOR FAMILY SECTION:

Page 39-Pitts   Issue of Taylor Blanton Doggett and Caitlin
Page 49-Pitts   McClelland Doggett:
Page 242-Taylor

Emerson Taylor Doggett, b. 22 Dec 2019. She is the great-granddaughter of Strother William (Ted) Lewis Jr. She is also the great-granddaughter of Mary Ann Taylor Doggett Nelson.

TAYLOR FAMILY SECTION:

Page 230   Robert Warren Reece, d. 5 Jul 2020. He is the son of Alberta Taylor Reece and Clarence Reece; buried in Signal Hill Memorial Park, Hanover, VA.